D1485415

IRON
&
SILK

HAMISH HAMILTON
LONDON

鍊
鬪
絲

IRON
&
SILK

Mark Salzman

Copyright © 1986 by Mark Salzman

First published in the United States 1987 by
Random House, Inc., New York, and simultaneously in Canada by
Random House of Canada Limited, Toronto.

First published in Great Britain 1987 by Hamish Hamilton Ltd
27 Wrights Lane London W8 5TZ

British Library Cataloguing in Publication Data

Salzman, Mark
Iron and silk.
1. China—Social life and customs—1976–
I. Title
951.05′8′0924   DS779.23

ISBN 0–241–12080–2

CALLIGRAPHY BY MARK SALZMAN

DESIGNED BY JOANNE METSCH

Printed and bound in Great Britain by
Butler & Tanner Ltd, Frome and London

Her swordplay moved the world.
Those who beheld her, numerous as the hills,
    lost themselves in wonder.
Heaven and Earth swayed in resonance . . .
Swift as the Archer shooting the nine suns,
She was exquisite, like a sky-god
    behind a team of dragons, soaring.

From "On Seeing a Pupil of Lady Kung-sun
Dance with the Sword," by Tu Fu, (712–70);
    translation by the author.

Contents

vii

Leaving

Arriving

For some reason I always had bad luck in Canton. In August 1984, on my way out of China after two years in Hunan Province, I was delayed at the Canton train station for half a day because of the seven-foot leather bag I carried. It contained five swords, four sabres, a staff, a halberd, two hooked swords, some knives and a nine-section steel whip. I had receipts and photos and a manila folder full of Foreign Affairs Bureau correspondence to prove that the weapons were all either gifts from my teachers or had been purchased in local stores, that none of them was an antique, and that I was the legitimate student of a well-known martial artist residing in Hunan, but the officials right away saw an opportunity to play their favorite game, Let's Make a Regulation.

"This bag is too long. You can't take it on the train. There's a regulation." We discussed this point for a while, and eventually the regulation was waived. "But these weapons are Chinese cultural artifacts. They cannot leave China, that's a regulation. You can take the bag, though." In time it was determined that the weapons might conceivably leave China, but I would need special permission from a certain office which would require a certain period of time to secure, so wouldn't I stay in Canton for a few days and come back with the proper documentation? My flight from Hong Kong to New York left in two days; I was desperate not to miss it. As I walked around the train station trying to think up a new strategy, I happened to bump into a Cantonese policeman I had met a year before. When I told him my problem he took me by the arm and led me back to the train station, where he began arguing on my behalf. He talked with the officials for over an hour about this and that, occasionally touching on the subject of my bag and its contents, then gently retreating to other matters. He eventually suggested that I give a short martial arts demonstration there in the train station— "Wouldn't that be fun?" He asked the people sitting on the long wooden benches in the station to make room for a performance, then helped them move the benches out of the way. I warmed up for a few minutes, took off my shoes and began a routine. Somewhere in mid-air my pants split wide open, from the base of the zipper to the belt line in back. A crowd of giggling old ladies rushed forward with needles and thread ready, followed by an equal number of old men with incurable illnesses who believed that I must have learned traditional medicine as part of my martial arts training, convincing the officials to let me through without further delay. The policeman helped me get on the train, then sat with me until it began to move. He hopped off, wished me well, then saluted as the train left the station.

I don't know exactly when the loudspeaker woke me up, but it was early, and the song was "Without the Communist Party, There Would Be No New China." I tried wrapping a pillow around my head, but one of the conductors tapped me on the knee and told me if I wanted any breakfast I'd better get to the dining car fast. It was 96 degrees already and rising. I stumbled over to a sink, splashed some water on my face, drank a few mouthfuls, then noticed the sign over the faucet —DON'T DRINK THIS. I found my way to the dining car and sat down with my three friends, Bob, Jean and Julian, also on their way into South Central China to teach English. An attendant urged us to try the Western style breakfast. It cost three times as much as the Chinese style breakfast, but I figured it might be the last Western food I would eat for some time, so I ordered it. It turned out to be a ham sandwich—a single slice of ham on two squares of dry bread, with no butter or mayonnaise, served with a warm glass of sweetened powdered milk. I heard a People's Liberation Army man behind me muttering to his friend, "Look at the foreigner—how can he eat that at seven in the morning?" After a few minutes the attendant returned and asked if I wanted the Western-style dessert, too. I said no, but that I would like to try the Chinese-style breakfast, a steaming bowl of noodles with a fried egg on top. "Ah yes! An international breakfast!" he said, and disappeared into the kitchen. "How can he eat so much?" the PLA man mumbled.

The four of us had had a difficult time in Canton the day before. A China Travel Service representative had approached

us as we got off the train from Hong Kong and insisted that
we would require his services if we expected to reach our
destinations in China. China Travel Service, China's only
travel service, specializes in imposing services on foreigners
and then failing to carry them out properly, thus creating a
need for more services. We would "need" a dolly to move our
bags from the customs office to the waiting room; once hired,
it turned out that the dolly could not leave the customs building parking lot, so we "had to" hire a taxi to carry them the
rest of the way. We would "have to" buy the most expensive
bunks on the train, since they were "the only seats left." The
CTS man led us to an empty waiting room and told us to sit
there and watch the luggage while he arranged everything.
My three companions, who had all lived or traveled in China
before, sensed disaster and insisted on going with him to the
ticket office. I did not feel like sitting alone with the bags in
that miserable room, so I asked Jean to stay with me.

Not long after Bob and Julian left with the CTS man, an
angry little woman in a blue uniform stalked in. "Where are
your tickets? What do you think you are doing here?" We
tried to explain that we didn't have any tickets, that a CTS
man had told us to wait there while he bought them for us,
but she would not let us even finish a sentence. "Where are
your tickets? You can't sit here if you don't have any tickets!
Let me see them." After several rounds of this, Jean and I
stopped answering her and stared at the floor in frustration.
The woman turned maroon, glared at us and marched out,
only to return after half an hour to repeat the interrogation.
This scene recurred four times over the next three and a half
hours, until at last Bob and Julian returned. At the ticket
office, the CTS man had tried to convince them that what he
meant was there were no tickets at all for that night, that we
had to buy the most expensive tickets on the next day's train

and spend the night in a foreigners' hotel in Canton. In the end, Bob and Julian managed to get the tickets for that night, but the CTS man had his revenge: just as we prepared to find a restaurant and buy some dinner, a Public Security Bureau official appeared with the CTS man and demanded to see our tickets and visas. He snapped them open and shut, then pointed at me. "You can go. Those three cannot." I asked why not.

"Your visa says you will be living in Changsha. Their visas say they will be living in Wuhan. But all of your tickets are for Changsha. They can't get on the train with faulty papers." We tried to explain that we all worked for the same organization, that my friends only wanted to help me settle for a day since I was new, and would then get back on the train for Wuhan, the next major stop on the line.

"You can't do that. There's a regulation."

He took them to the Public Security Bureau office, leaving me alone with the bags in the room. The angry woman in the blue uniform showed up again and demanded to see my ticket. I showed it to her, and she demanded to see my friends' tickets as well. "They have them," I answered. "Then you'll have to move their bags out of here," she snapped.

Five minutes before the train left, Bob, Jean and Julian came running back into the waiting room with little permission slips. We grabbed our bags and ran across the monstrous platform, with the Chinese national anthem blaring over the loudspeakers. I got into the train first, opened a window and had them throw the bags in to me. They jumped on, and the train began to move.

After breakfast I heard over the loudspeaker a flourish of trumpets and a woman's voice, quivering with emotion: "Comrades—we have arrived! Changsha—a city with a long

7

and glorious history . . ." I looked out the window and saw in the distance a sprawling cluster of cement buildings, and a group of peasants walking alongside the railroad tracks with a huge pig tied to a wheelbarrow that had a wooden wheel. In direct sunlight, at 97 degrees, they wore heavy black cotton jackets and pants that looked like quilts for all the patches sewn on them. The transition from countryside to city was abrupt: one moment we saw rice paddies, vegetable patches and fishponds, and several hundred yards later the train came to a halt in Changsha, a city of more than one million people and the capital of Hunan Province.

We unloaded our bags out the window, since the aisle was jammed with people shoving to get off or on, then stood with our mountain of luggage in the sweltering heat as a growing crowd of peasants, mouths agape, formed a tight circle around us. They were brusquely scattered by three somber men in Mao suits who strode up to us, determined that we were the right foreigners, then assumed postures and expressions that indicated warm, heartfelt greetings. Long handshakes occurred, and they identified themselves as members of the Foreign Affairs Bureau of Hunan Medical College: Comrade Hu, Comrade Lin and Group Leader Chen. Comrade Hu spoke English, and although all four of us spoke Chinese, he insisted on speaking English while the other two Foreign Affairs men smiled broadly, nodded and occasionally said, "Ah, ha ha!" Comrade Hu frowned with concentration and delivered a speech. "We are responsible for the safety and convenience of foreigners. On behalf of our college, we warmly welcome you. And now, let's go."

The Foreign Affairs team led us into the station and helped us carry our bags down a broken escalator into the main concourse, the largest empty room I have ever seen. The Changsha train station was built toward the end of the Cultural Revolution to accommodate the hordes of pilgrims who came every day to visit Chairman Mao's birthplace near Changsha. By the time construction ended, however, interest in the Chairman had waned, and since Changsha is neither a scenic nor an important city, hardly anyone stops there anymore.

A white van waited for us in front of the station. Its driver, an overweight fellow from North China, ran to greet us and shook all our hands for a long time, then helped load our things into the van. He started the engine, held his palm against the horn and gave it a long blast to warm it up, then shot full speed into the crowded streets. He swerved and braked violently to avoid pedestrians who darted into the road without looking, swarms of bicyclists who rode in the middle of the street, trucks, jeeps and huge buses that careened as if driven by madmen, and long carts piled sometimes ten feet high with construction materials, furniture, or tubs of human excrement, which were pulled by men dressed in rags, the veins of their necks and calves bulging from the strain. At no time during this ordeal was our horn silent, nor was that of any other vehicle on the road, rendering them all essentially useless. I asked Comrade Hu why the driver held the horn down like that, and he answered, without a trace of irony in his voice, "Traffic Safety."

Small shops lined the streets, all with their doors propped open, so I was able to catch glimpses of carpenters, woolspinners, key makers, bicycle repairmen, cooks and tailors, all working in rooms lit by a single bare bulb, using tools I had seen before only in antique shops or museums. In front of the shops, families of several generations sat on bamboo chairs and beds pulled out onto the sidewalk, fanning themselves, holding infants who urinated into the street, and playing cards.

It was all a bit shocking, but most shocking was how filthy

everything looked. I had heard that China was spotlessly clean. Instead, dishwater and refuse were thrown casually out of windows, rats the size of squirrels could be seen flattened out all over the roads, spittle and mucus lay everywhere, and the dust and ash from coal-burning stoves, heaters and factories mixed with dirt and rain to stain the entire city an unpleasant greyish-brown. The smell of nightsoil, left in shallow outhouse troughs for easy collection, wafted through the streets and competed with the unbelievable din of automobile horns to offend the senses. No one that I could see was smiling, or had red cheeks, as all the Chinese do in *China Reconstructs* magazine.

We reached the college, passing through an iron gate into a walled compound that contained more walls and gates, and some buildings. All the buildings were of grey concrete except for a few red brick ones, most of which were in the process of being either torn down or plastered with concrete so as to look "modern." The entire campus seemed mired in a swamp of loose bricks, cinderblocks and grey mud. I asked Comrade Hu why there wasn't any grass on the ground. "Grass makes mosquitoes," he answered. The van moved toward a two-story brick house, where a group of older men in tailored Mao jackets stood in a loose circle, looking none too happy in the stupefying heat. When our van approached they all stiffened and broke into smiles, extending their hands to shake even before the van had come to a stop. A complicated flurry of introductions ensued, none of which I could absorb except that these were important people in the administration of the college, and they were all convinced that the deep friendship and understanding that already existed between us would become even deeper with time. As I shook hands with one of the leaders, Comrade Lin suddenly hawked as if clearing his entire chest cavity and sent a lump of mucus behind me onto a brick a few feet away. I desperately wanted to laugh out loud, but no one even blinked, so neither did I. "The Chinese and American peoples have a long history of mutual friendship and cooperative teamwork," the leader said. "I am sure your stay here will prove educational to us both."

The leaders said that I must surely be tired from my journey, so they left me to settle into my new home. Comrade Hu led me into the house and pointed to my room. A four foot seven, sturdy-looking peasant woman in her late fifties sat inside. As soon as I came into view, she jumped straight up and ran at me, greeting me in Changsha dialect so loudly I thought her voice would knock me down. "This is Comrade Yang," Comrade Hu told me. "Everyone calls her Old Yang. Her name means 'sheep.' She cleans the house and boils the water. If you need anything, let her know." Old Sheep laughed in shrieks and ran to pick up my bags. The largest of them, my cello case, stood as tall as she, but she insisted on leaning it against her back and carrying it into the room.

I lay down on my bed, a wooden frame with a bamboo mat spread over it, and balanced an electric fan on my stomach so it would blow on my face. Even in my underwear I was sweating heavily, but the fan made me comfortable. Suddenly it stopped working. I got up and fiddled with the plug, to no avail, then put on some clothes and went outside. Old Sheep was hanging her laundry to dry on lines she stretched from the bars on my window to the cement wall surrounding our house. (The college built this wall, I was told, for the convenience of the American teachers, as it would protect us from "bad elements" who might come to bother us. By unfortunate coincidence, it also protected us from good elements such as our Chinese students and friends, who felt uneasy passing through the conspicuous iron gate that led into our compound.) I told Old Sheep about the fan and she laughed,

"Of course! The electricity is off!" I asked her how often that happened. "Sometimes every day, sometimes every other day, but sometimes we go for days without a blackout! Don't worry, it will only be for a little while." Then she asked me if I was thirsty, and when I told her I was, she trotted into the house and came back with a glass of boiling water. "Do you want tea leaves in this?" "No, thank you."

That afternoon at exactly three o'clock, when *xiuxi*, the Chinese version of siesta, ends, Comrade Hu called my friends and me out of the house. "Now it is time for recreational activities. We will show you the scenic spots and places of revolutionary interest in Changsha." We got into the van again, joining a few doctors from the college, and went for another hair-raising trip through downtown Changsha. We drove up Yuelu Mountain and visited the gravesites of several tens of local revolutionary heroes, then stopped at the Mawangdui museum, which contains spectacular cultural artifacts and the two-thousand-year-old preserved corpse of a marquise of the Han dynasty, all dug up out of nearby Mawangdui tomb. While I was looking at the corpse, one of the doctors told me that when it was first discovered it was in perfect condition. "But at that time, during the 'so-called Cultural Revolution,' bad leftist elements led by the Gang of Four were in power, so when the body was unearthed it was declared a relic of the feudal past, and was left in the sun to rot while peasants and workers threw stones at it. Isn't that awful?" he asked, smiling.

Last of all, we went to see the tomb site where the marquise had lain for so many years before being discovered by the citizens of New China and brought to justice at last. Over a small hill, we came to a huge rain shelter. Under the shelter was a deep hole. "This is the hole," said Comrade Hu. "If you like, I can take a picture of you standing in front of it, so you will never forget it."

As soon as we got back home I realized that I had terrible diarrhea, which was to plague me for the next three weeks. I had no appetite for dinner, but did manage to eat some rice and wash it down with some water that Old Sheep set out on a table for the afternoon so it might cool to room temperature. Just as we finished eating, Comrade Hu appeared in the dining hall. "And now, please, it is time for entertainment. Will you follow me?" The van picked us up once more and took us to the Hunan Theater, a huge, Soviet-looking building on the main street of town, May First Road. That night a troupe of performers from Congo sang and danced to promote friendship between China and Congo. The jammed theater was unbearably hot and stuffy, and reeked of sweat. The audience talked, walked around and spat loudly throughout the performance, so loudly during a mouth harp piece that the musicians gave up halfway through the song and stepped off stage. The performance came to a rousing finale when a striking black man dressed in a studded white body suit unbuttoned to his navel slid across the stage on his knees, threw his head back with abandon and sang out, "Africa—I love you!" in Chinese. At that point, all the Africans came onstage to sing together, where they were joined by a group of aging Hunan Province officials. The Africans, dressed in colorful native costumes, swayed and clapped as they sang a Chinese song—"Socialism is Good"—while the cadres, all dressed in identical grey Mao suits, stood motionless in front of them.

When the song was finished, a little Chinese girl with painted red cheeks came out with a bouquet of flowers, which she presented to the man in the white Elvis costume. The singer lifted her up in his arms and kissed her, whereupon she became frightened and tried to wriggle free. The cadres turned around to face the singers and shake hands. At that moment, the curtain fell—right onto the heads of the cadres, sending one of their Mao caps rolling across the stage. A roar of laughter and applause rose up from the audience, and the entertainment had come to an end.

A Piano

Teacher Wei

Hong Kong Foot

Myopia

I'd been interested in China since I was thirteen. I had seen the television movie *Kung Fu* and decided right away that peace of mind and a shaved head were what I had always wanted. My parents supported my interest, buying all sorts of books about kung fu and Chinese art for me; they even enrolled me in a kung fu school, although they did not let me shave my head. I practiced several hours a day, tried to overcome pain by walking to school barefoot in the snow, and let my kung fu teacher pound me senseless in cemeteries at night so that I might learn to "die well." I enjoyed all of this so much that my interest continued through high school, and spread to wanting to learn Chinese painting and calligraphy and then the language itself.

I went to Yale and majored in Chinese literature. By the time I finished college, I was fluent in Mandarin and nearly so in Cantonese, had struggled through a fair amount of classical Chinese and had translated the works of a modern poet. Oddly, though, I had no desire to go to China; it sounded like a giant penal colony to me, and besides, I have never liked traveling much. I did need a job, though, so I applied to and was accepted by the Yale-China Association to teach English at Hunan Medical College in Changsha from August 1982 to July 1984.

The college assigned three classes to me: twenty-six doctors and teachers of medicine, four men and one woman identified as "the Middle-Aged English Teachers," and twenty-five medical students ranging in age from twenty-two to twenty-eight. First I met the doctors, who stood up to applaud my entrance into the classroom and remained standing while the Class Monitor read a prepared statement that welcomed and praised me.

Their English ability ranged from nearly fluent to practically hopeless. At the end of the first week of classes the Class Monitor read aloud the results of their "Suggestions for Better Study" meeting: "Dear Teacher Mark. You are an active boy! Your lessons are very humorous and very wonderful. To improve our class, may we suggest that in the future we (1) spend more time reading, (2) spend more time listening, (3) spend more time writing and (4) spend more time speaking. Also, some students feel you are moving too quickly through the book. However, some students request that you speed up a little, because the material is too elementary. We hope we can struggle together to overcome these contradictions! Thank you, our dear teacher."

I was next introduced to the medical students, whom I taught only once a week, on Tuesday nights. They were nearly faint with excitement over meeting a foreign teacher; when I first walked into the room they didn't move or breathe, and no one dared look directly at me. The Monitor yelled, "Stand up!" and they rose with such formality that I did not know how to respond. At last I saluted them gravely and yelled in Chinese, "Sit down!" They looked stunned, then exploded into cheers, giving me the thumbs-up sign and speaking to me all at once in Chinese. It seemed that the tension had been released, so when they calmed down I asked them to intro-

duce themselves in English. At first they giggled and whispered to one another, then slowly they lowered their heads,
turned pale and went mute.

That night when I got back to the house I found a note on
my door from Teacher Wu, a senior member of the English
Department, asking me to see her in her office the next morning. I went to bed feeling uneasy, wondering if I had done or
said something wrong during the past week and was about to
be purged or criticized.

The offices and classrooms of the Foreign Languages Department were on the second floor of a three-story building.
The first floor housed cadavers for the Anatomy Department
and the third floor was occupied by the Political and Moral
Education Department. Students used to joke that it was hard
to determine who slept more soundly in that building—the
bodies, or the students on the third floor. I groped up the
unlit staircase and found Teacher Wu in her office, surrounded by piles of paper that turned out to be the draft of
an application for a World Bank loan that the college had
given her to translate into English. She pointed to a seat next
to her and asked if I would go over the translation with her
to check for mistakes. She handed me two piles: the Chinese
version, and a copy of her translation—all handwritten, since
the college had only one copying machine and the only
authorized operator was on vacation.

Nearly seventy years old, Teacher Wu was short and plump,
with heavy eyelids above and below her eyes that made her
look tired. I had heard that both she and her husband had
received advanced degrees from an American university in
the 1940's. When they finished they returned to China, determined to serve their country whatever the outcome of the
civil war. Like most Chinese with intellectual backgrounds,

they were to suffer despite their patriotism. Teacher Wu's husband came under attack during the Anti-Rightist Campaign in the late 1950's; to protect his family, he apologized to the State for his "crimes against Socialism," then took his own life. During the Cultural Revolution Teacher Wu became a target and had to endure not only her own public denouncement and humiliation but those of her son, who was "sent down" to the countryside for nearly a decade.

I sat down next to her and began to look over the English version of the text:

"III. GOALS

1. The money lent by the World Bank would be used to improve the general quality of teaching and treatment at Hunan Medical College in order to bring about the realization of the goal of realizing the Four Modernizations by the year 2000.

2. These funds would aid in the enrichment of our programs here at Hunan Medical College in the fields of education and health, so that we may better serve our Motherland.

3. With the purchase of new classroom materials and laboratory equipment, we could improve the overall quality of the curriculum at Hunan Medical College.

"IV. CONCLUSIONS

1. That the acquisition of new and vital tools, such as microscopes, earphones, spectrographs, etc., is a necessary step toward the realization of the goal of realizing the Four Modernizations by the year 2000 according to the directives of the Party as set forth in the New Constitution of the Twelfth Party Congress of the Chinese Communist Party."

And so on.

I looked at her and didn't know what to say. Could she really think that this was appropriate wording for an application to an international lending group? I finally asked her as much. She did not look up from her work. "Mm. Is there something wrong with the grammar?" I said no, the grammar seemed fine, but the content seemed a bit weak, perhaps. Her expression did not change at all. "But this is a translation of the text written by the officials of our college. This is the Chinese way of writing this sort of thing. I am only an English teacher, I cannot presume to change it." I told her that perhaps from a Chinese point of view this kind of language was acceptable, but that from a Western point of view it seemed repetitive, and since they were applying to an institution run according to Western principles, they might want to draft a more Western-sounding text. She sighed, still without looking at me, and said nothing. I got the impression that she was quietly hoping I wouldn't press the issue, so I didn't, and pointed out a misspelling.

We corrected misspellings for about an hour, then took a break for tea. "Have you met the Middle-Aged English Teachers yet?" she asked. I said I hadn't. "Mm. They are a special group. Originally they were Russian teachers, but then, because of certain political conditions, Russian teachers became English teachers." She paused to refill my teacup, closed her eyes for a moment, then continued. "Then, during the Cultural Revolution, as you surely know, all teaching was interrupted. There is no need to go into that. Anyway, now we are all teaching again. The Middle-Aged English Teachers are victims of the Gang of Four; now they think they are too old to improve. You may find it difficult to inspire them to work"—she laughed—"but they are a humorous group. I think you will like them."

We worked on the application until lunch time, when she suggested that we walk home together, since her apartment was not far from where I lived. When we reached her building she said, "By the way, I hear you brought a cello with you. Why don't you bring it here, to my house, tonight? I used to be a musician myself—I would love to hear it."

After dinner I carried my cello to her building. It was the first time I had entered a Chinese person's home. She lived in a tiny apartment that she shared with "Auntie Tan," an old woman from the countryside who helped with the shopping, cooking and clearning. The apartment had cement walls, bare except for a calendar and a few photographs, a bare cement floor, a bare light bulb in each room, and sparse furnishings, with one exception: against one wall stood an upright piano.

I asked her how she had managed to get a piano, and she said that she grew up playing and had continued to study when she was in America. She bought the piano there, and brought it back to China when she returned with her husband. "I haven't had much time to practice it since then, but nowadays I try to play whenever I have free time." She went over, opened it up, and began to play.

The piano was badly damaged—many of the notes did not sound, and those that did were so out of tune I almost wished they hadn't. She invited me to play a duet with her, but we had to give up. After a pause she sighed and said quietly, "One night the Red Guards came. They took everything in the house out and burned it. They wanted to take the piano, too, but"—and here she smiled at the floor—"it was too heavy for them to throw out the window! So they just hit it for a while and left. I haven't been able to find anyone to fix it since then." I said I wished that I could help her, but though my mother played the piano I had never learned to tune or repair one.

"Your mother is a pianist?"

"Well, she was a pianist. Now she plays the harpsichord."

"Mm. So you know what a piano should sound like, then? You grew up hearing it every day, didn't you?"

"Yes."

"Mm."

The next day I went to meet the Middle-Aged English Teachers. They had drawn an elaborate mural on the blackboard in several colors of chalk, composed of the words "Welcome Teacher Mark!" surrounded by an assortment of animals, musical notes and Chinese characters, and had set out candies on my desk along with a cup of tea and a thermos of hot water. When I walked in they stood up and stepped forward to shake my hand—all except for Teacher Du, the one woman in the group, who covered her mouth with her hand and smiled shyly. Since they had had American teachers already, they were more relaxed than the other groups. I introduced myself and told them a few stories about my family and friends, and they laughed uproariously at the funny parts. They even interrupted me a few times to ask questions or to accuse me of exaggerating, which came as a great relief after a week of stiff formality.

I asked them to introduce themselves to me, but they chose instead to introduce the person sitting next to them. Teacher Xu began: "Teacher Cai was a wonderful dancer when he was a young man. He is famous in our college, because he has a beautiful wife." Teacher Cai hit Teacher Xu and said, "Teacher Xu is always late to class, and he is afraid of his wife!" "I am not!" "Oh, but you are!" Teacher Zhang pointed to Teacher Zhu. "Teacher Zhu was a Navy man. But he can't swim! And Teacher Du is very fat. So we call her Fatty Du— she has the most powerful voice in our college!" Fatty Du beamed with pride and said, "And Teacher Zhang's special characteristic is that he is afraid of me!" "I am not!" "Oh, but you are!"

As Teacher Wu had predicted, I liked this group very much, though when I assigned them reading and a short composition for the next class they became quiet and looked less cheerful than before.

A week later Teacher Wu appeared at my door early in the morning, breathless with excitement. "I have something here . . ." and she pulled out of her bag something that looked like a bent screwdriver. "I heard that an orchestra was passing through Changsha, so I found them and talked to them. Their pianist had one of these—it is a tuning wrench. He said I can have it until tonight—can you try?"

"Try what?"

"To tune it—tune the piano!"

"But I don't know how."

"Try!"

I asked her not to stay in the apartment while I worked, because it would only make me more nervous, so she prepared a thermos of tea and promised me a good dinner that evening. "And if you need anything, just tell Auntie Tan—she'll be right in the kitchen." Auntie Tan gave me a toothless smile and nodded, and I smiled back.

After Teacher Wu left I began to disassemble the piano. As I was taking off one of the boards concealing the pedal mechanism, I heard a loud squeak and a frantic scratching. I stepped back and watched three large rodents scurry out of the piano, around the room and down a drainpipe.

Using sandpaper and a pair of pliers I managed to get all the hammers loose, and I repaired the pedal system by replacing the broken levers with several wooden rulers that I connected with nuts and bolts. To tune the instrument I damped two of the strings of each note with my thumb and forefinger while I adjusted the third, then tuned each of the others to it. Since I have only semi-perfect pitch, I set middle C according to a Michael Jackson tape played through my Walkman.

I finished just before dinner. I was terribly excited and went into the kitchen to announce my success to Auntie Tan, but saw that she had stuffed her ears with balls of cotton, over which she had tied a thick towel, and seemed to be taking a nap. Teacher Wu arrived shortly thereafter, but did not yet go near the piano. "Let's eat first," she said.

We had a delicious meal of smoked eggs, noodles with pork strips in broth, and a whole chicken—a real luxury in China, only for special occasions—stewed in a thick yellow sauce. Then we had tea and popsicles that Auntie Tan had bought for us in the street. At last Teacher Wu sat down at the piano, took out several books of music, and began to play. She played through a few pieces and played them beautifully, but said nothing for a long time. Finally she stopped playing, looked directly at me, and said in Chinese, "Thank you very much."

I stood up and said that she was very welcome, but that I had some work to do and should be getting back to the house. She shifted into the rituals of seeing off a guest, which involve pleading with the guest to stay, offering him tea and candies, then accompanying him at least part of his way home. This time she walked me all the way to my door. As she turned to go back, she said, "In your next letter to your mother, tell her you fixed a piano in China for an old lady." Then she went home.

I did not like riding the buses in Changsha; they were always terribly crowded, sometimes with passengers squeezed part-way out of the doors and windows. I once rode a bus which stopped at a particularly crowded streetcorner. Women were holding their children above their heads so they would not be crushed in the shoving, and I saw a man desperately grab onto something inside the bus while most of his body was not yet on board. The bus attendant screamed at him to let go, but he would not, so she pressed the button operating the doors and they crashed shut on him, fixing him exactly half inside and half out. The bus proceeded to its destination, where-upon the doors opened and the man stepped down, cheerfully paid the attendant half the usual fare, and went on his way.

To avoid having to ride the buses, I decided to follow the example of the three senior Yale-China teachers in Changsha, Bill, Bob and Marcy, and buy a bicycle. Because I was a for-eigner, I was allowed to choose the model I wanted, pay for it on the spot with foreign currency certificates and take it home right away. I walked it out of the store with most of the store following me, got on, and rode away feeling acutely self-conscious, as if I had walked into a car dealer, paid for a Porsche in cash, and driven it out of the showroom right through the floor-to-ceiling windows.

When I got back to the house I felt grimy from all the dust on the roads, so I went upstairs to take a bath. Foreigners were not supposed to take showers in the public bathhouse, so our building was equipped with its own bathtub on the second floor, with an electric water heater attached to the wall above it. The hot water passed from the tank, which was at head level, through an iron pipe into the tub. The first time I used the tub, not realizing that the iron pipe conducted the heat of the heating element, I leaned my backside against it while drying off. As soon as the pain struck I reached out and grabbed the only object within reach—the wire supplying electricity to the heater, which stretched across the room over the tub. As soon as I had pulled myself free, I remembered my parents' command never to touch wires or electrical devices when standing in a bathtub. I let go in a panic, lost my balance and fell back onto the pipe. After that I got in the habit of drying off in my room.

This time, as I ran downstairs with a towel around my waist, I was met in my room by Teacher Wu and a silver-haired lady who looked about the same age as Teacher Wu, but was very thin and had fiercely bright eyes. Teacher Wu, who seemed not to notice that I was half-naked and dripping wet, introduced us.

"Mark, this is Teacher Wei, my colleague. The college has assigned her to be your teacher, in case you would like to continue your study of Chinese. Since you have a background in classical Chinese, she offered to teach you; she taught classical Chinese in our middle school here for many years. She is a very good teacher." Teacher Wei shook her head and said, "No, no. I'm a bad teacher," but she grinned. Teacher Wu wanted to arrange a schedule then and there, but Teacher Wei pulled her out of the room saying, "He's wet now. I will come again some other time." She looked at me. "I will come tomorrow and bring the books you will need."

After they left I remembered that I had met Teacher Wei before, at a welcoming party thrown the day after I arrived.

One of the Middle-Aged English Teachers had taken me aside and said, "Teacher Wei is a widow and has the reputation of being the strictest teacher in our college. It is said that she never smiles and has never laughed out loud!"

I did not have much time to worry about how I would get along with mirthless Teacher Wei, however—that night I was scheduled to give a lecture for which I had yet to prepare. My predecessors at the college had begun a Wednesday night "Western Culture Lecture Series" held in the largest hall in the college and open to anyone interested in learning English. Virtually everyone in our college was interested in learning English, so we usually drew a crowd of three to five hundred. Past topics had ranged from "Medical Schools in America" to "The American Legal System," and each lecture, an hour and a half in length, was given twice—once to the doctors and teachers and once to the students. I was to give my first lecture that night to the doctors and teachers; my topic was *"E.T."*

For starters, I wrote out the events of the movie as I remembered them. Then I figured out what vocabulary I would have to introduce—like "spaceship," "alien," "ouch" and "phone home." I adopted a distinct facial expression, walk, or tone of voice for each character, to make it easier for the audience to know right away who was who, and decided to alternate between narrating and acting out the scenes. I worried that the audience might not appreciate this sort of storytelling and think it childish or uninteresting, but I did not have to worry long. When I introduced E.T. by jumping on the lab table and hopping the length of it with my knees under my chin and my hands dragging on the table, the audience rose to its feet and cheered.

The next day Teacher Wei arrived after xiuxi with a cloth

bag and her glasses case. She walked into my room, sat down and accepted a cup of tea, put on her glasses, and took a book from her bag.

"We'll begin with this collection of classical essays prepared for Chinese high school students." She handed it to me and took out another copy for herself. I noticed that her copy was filled with pencil notes, smudged from her habit of following the text with her fingertip as she read.

"We'll begin with an essay by Tao Qian. You are familiar with him, aren't you? Then of course you know that he was a hermit and a famous drinker, almost fifteen hundred years ago. Most of the great Chinese authors were drinkers and dreamers."

She stopped, took off her glasses, and looked closely at me.

"I saw your lecture last night, the one called 'E.T.' You are a very naughty boy!" She took from her bag a small medicine jar and handed it to me. I opened it and found that it contained a shot of *baijiu*—Chinese rice liquor.

"Since we will be reading the works of drinkers and dreamers, and since you are clearly an eccentric yourself, I think it only fitting that you appreciate their essays like this. From now on I will bring a small bottle of baijiu when I come. You will finish it, then we will have our lesson."

I thought she was kidding, so I laughed, but she really meant for me to drink it. She reached into her bag and pulled out a container of fried peanuts, still warm from the wok.

"You must have something to eat with it, of course. I brought some peanuts for you. If you don't finish the wine, no lesson for you."

I finished the baijiu and peanuts, to her great satisfaction. Then she put on her glasses and began the lesson.

. . .

Not long after our first lesson Teacher Wei happened to walk by our house while I was practicing *wushu* out front. *Wushu* is the Chinese word for martial arts, and refers to any of hundreds of schools of armed and unarmed combat practiced in China for more than two thousand years. These schools range from the slow, graceful Taijiquan, or T'ai Chi Ch'uan, to the explosive Northern and Southern schools of Shaolin boxing. In the West, Chinese martial arts are called "kung fu" or "gong fu," but the word *gong fu* actually means skill that transcends mere surface beauty. A martial artist whose technique is decorative but without power "has no gong fu," whereas, say, a calligrapher whose work is not pretty to look at but reflects a strong, austere taste certainly "has gong fu."

Teacher Wei walked over and asked what I was doing. When I told her that wushu had been an interest of mine for many years, she nodded with approval.

"In classical Chinese we have a saying that to be a true gentleman it is important to be 'well-versed in the literary and the martial.' Wushu is an excellent sport. Have you found a teacher here yet?"

At this I became very excited. I told her that I would love to find a teacher but had no idea where to look for one, and that even if I found one, I wouldn't know how to approach him. I also expressed my doubts that a wushu teacher would accept a foreign student, as I had heard that they were usually secretive and old-fashioned in their thinking. She shook her head vigorously.

"That may be true of the mediocre fighters, but you will find that the best fighters in China are not superstitious or close-minded. If you want to learn wushu, you will have a teacher—I can guarantee it, because you are a friendly boy. That is most important. Besides,"—she allowed herself a giggle—"you are exotic. Your big nose alone will open doors! You have blond hair, blue eyes, and you are very strong— you're a 'model foreigner!' Teachers will find you." I asked her if she knew anyone who might be able to help me, but she just smiled and said to be patient, then continued on her way.

As I walked back into the house to take a bath and have breakfast, I noticed a man with close-cropped white hair squatting on the steps of our building. I said good morning to him and he answered politely, complimenting my Chinese. I asked him if he had come to see one of the American teach- ers, and he said no, then explained that he was staying in the one empty room in our building, which the college offered to guests when the regular guest house was full. He was a doctor of rehabilitative therapy and traditional Chinese medicine at a hospital on the outskirts of the city, and had come to repre- sent his specialty at a conference our college was sponsoring. His name was Dr. Li. When he stood up to introduce himself, I noticed that he was taller than I, had broad shoulders, and held back his head slightly, which gave him an extraordinarily distinguished appearance.

"I saw you exercising," he said, "and overheard your con- versation with the lady. There are several good teachers in Hunan."

"Do you know any of them?"

"Yes, I know one or two."

"Do you think any of them would be willing to teach me?"

"Hard to say," he said, then wished me good morning and left for breakfast.

Dr. Li stayed for one week. Every morning he squatted in front of the house, watched me exercise, talked for a little while, then left to get breakfast. The afternoon before he left he happened to return to the house while I was sitting out front working on a charcoal and ink sketch. He sat next to me until I finished, then took it in his hands to have a better look. He seemed to like it, so I asked him please to keep it.

"Thank you very much—it is a beautiful drawing," he said, then got up to leave. "Will you be exercising tomorrow morning?" he asked casually.

"Probably."

"I'll tell you something. The reason you haven't seen anyone practicing wushu is that you get up too late. You are out here at 6:30 every morning. The wushu people have already finished practicing by then! Get up a little earlier tomorrow; you might see something then." He thanked me again for the drawing and went into the house.

At five o'clock the next morning my alarm went off. I scrambled outside and sat down on the steps. It was still dark out, and I didn't see anyone else up yet, much less practicing wushu. Then it occurred to me how unlikely it would be for a wushu expert to choose to practice in the north campus of Hunan Medical College, and I cursed myself for not asking Dr. Li where I should go. I stood up to go back to bed when I noticed an unfamiliar shape next to a bamboo tree planted against the south end of the house. I walked over and saw that it was Dr. Li, balanced on one leg in an impossible posture, his body so still I could not even see him breathe.

After an interminable length of time he suddenly straightened up, nodding to acknowledge my presence. He then practiced a Taijiquan form that lasted some twenty minutes. He moved so slowly I felt hypnotized watching him. When he finished, he gestured for me to stand next to him.

"Of the wushu I practice," he said, "my favorite is called the Xuan Men Sword. *Xuan* means dark, or mysterious; *men* means gate." He had me stay put while he quickly found two

sticks of equal length, perhaps two and a half feet long, then
gave one to me.

"Do what I do," he said, and began teaching me the form.

After half an hour or so, he said it was time for breakfast
and told me that this was the last day he would be living in
our house, so unfortunately he could not teach me every
morning.

"But I will come here every three days or so until you learn
the form. Wait for me here, in front of your house, early in
the morning."

He kept his promise and I was able to learn all the movements of the form in a month, but he insisted that something
was still missing. Although I performed the techniques well,
he could see I was not concentrating in a manner appropriate
for the form: "You look good, but you have no gong fu." At
last he invited me to his home for dinner, saying that he could
teach me better there. When I followed the directions he gave
me to his house, I realized that he had been riding forty-five
minutes each way to teach me for the past month. He lived
well outside the center of the city on a small hill surrounded
by lush, irrigated fields. As soon as I arrived his wife offered
me a hot towel to wipe the dust off my hands and face. The
three of us sat down to a simple but delicious meal of pork
strips over noodles in broth, steamed fish, and plenty of rice.

When we had finished, Dr. Li's wife took what was left over
and carried it into the adjacent bedroom where, I discovered,
his son and two daughters, all in their teens or twenties, were
sitting. When I asked why they hadn't eaten with us, Dr. Li
seemed puzzled. "That would be rude, wouldn't it? You are
our guest, after all."

He apparently sensed my discomfort, because he invited
them to join us for dessert—a few oranges and apples, and
more tea. Dr. Li's children were far too shy to carry on a

conversation with me, but one of them did manage to ask me if American food was the same as Chinese food. I tried to describe a typical American meal for them, but it proved difficult: how do you explain pizza to someone who has never seen cheese, tomato sauce, or a pie crust?

After dessert Dr. Li took two swords from another room, tied them together with some string, and asked me to follow him. We got on our bicycles and rode to nearby Mawangdui, the site of the hole that had contained the two-thousand-year-old corpse. We walked past that hole to a second mound, which Dr. Li told me was supposed to contain the tomb of either the marquise's husband or her son. The top of the mound was nearly flat and had patches of grass growing here and there on its packed dirt surface. As Dr. Li unfastened the two swords and handed me one, I realized that the flat part of the mound was just the right size for the form he had taught me.

The sun had not yet gone down, and it cast a glittering reflection over the Xiang River a few miles away. The vegetable plots in all directions around us caught the light as well and glowed brightly, in sharp contrast to the deep red earth of the paths between the fields.

"Just think," he said, "under your feet is so much history! There are all sorts of treasures in this mound—probably even swords like these, only real ones that were used in ancient wars. With all this history under you, don't you feel moved? Now, practice the form, and this time don't fuss over the technique. Just enjoy it, as if this mound gave you power. That is the kind of feeling that makes wushu beautiful—it is tradition passing through you. Isn't that a kind of power?"

After the lesson at Mawangdui Dr. Li said there was no need for him to come in the mornings to teach me anymore, but that if I wanted any further instruction I could visit him any-time. Since very few people in China have telephones, about the only way to arrange to visit someone is to walk to his house and knock on the door. If it's a friend, you can often dispense with the knocking and just walk in. My students told me again and again that if I ever wanted to see them I could walk into their homes any time of day or night.

"But what if you are busy?"

"It doesn't matter! If you come, I won't be busy anymore!"

"But what if you are asleep?"

"Then wake me up!"

No matter how often I was given these instructions, though, I could not bring myself to follow them. Whenever someone banged on my door unexpectedly, or simply appeared in my room, I always felt slightly nervous, and I only visited my friends when I felt I had a good reason.

So I did not call upon Dr. Li for more lessons, but con-tented myself with practicing the Xuan Men Sword and trying to recreate the feeling invoked by dancing with the sword on the Han dynasty tomb.

By that time Teacher Wei was helping me through a classi-cal novel, *The Water Margin*, the story of a hundred and eight renegade heroes, all martial arts experts, who band to-gether and perform deeds similar to those of Robin Hood and the men of Sherwood Forest. Teacher Wei and I agreed that our favorite character was Lu Zhishen, known as the Phony Monk, a man with a righteous soul but a powerful temper, who was on the run from the law after killing an evil mer-chant to redress an injustice. To escape execution he became a Buddhist monk, but was unsuited to the monk's abstemious way of life. He would sneak out of the monastery at night to drink superhuman amounts of baijiu and eat roast dogs, bones and all, then return to the monastery where the other monks would scold him for drinking and eating meat. In a drunken rage, he would beat them all up, reduce a few buildings to rubble, then throw up in the meditation hall. Of course, the next day he would feel very bad and fix everything he had broken.

My lessons with Teacher Wei had come to involve more than reading and writing assignments. She was a teacher in the Chinese tradition, taking responsibility not only for my academic progress but for my development as a person. She had advice for me concerning my family and friends, my diet, my clothing, my study and exercise habits, and my attitude toward life. At times I got impatient with her and explained that in America, children become adults around the time they leave for college and like to make decisions for themselves after that. She was appalled. "Don't your parents and teachers care about you?"

"Of course they do, but—"

"Then how can they leave you stranded when you are only a child?"

"Well, we—"

"And how can you possibly think you understand everything? You are only twenty-two years old! You are so far away from home, and I am your teacher; if I don't care about you, won't you be lonely?"

She pointed out that the close relationship between teacher and student has existed in China since before the time of Confucius and should not be underestimated—besides, she was older than me and knew better. I couldn't help respecting her conviction, and she seemed to get such pleasure out of trying to figure and then to straighten me out that I stopped resisting and let her educate me.

I learned how to dress to stay comfortable throughout the

year (a useful skill in a place without air conditioning or heat in most buildings), how to prevent and treat common illness, how to behave toward teachers, students, strangers and bureaucrats, how to save books from mildew and worms, and never to do anything to excess.

"Mark, you laugh a great deal during your lectures. Why?"

"Because, Teacher Wei, I am having fun."

"I see. Laugh less. It seems odd that a man laughs so hard at his own jokes. People think you are a bit crazy, or perhaps choking."

"Teacher Wei, do you think it is bad to laugh?"

"No, not at all. In fact, it is healthy to laugh. In Chinese we have a saying that if you laugh you will live long. But you shouldn't laugh too much, or you will have digestive problems."

Teacher Wei also encouraged me to travel. She knew I was homesick; she said that travel gives experience, helps cope with sadness, and in any case is fun. I disagreed with her. My last trip, from Hong Kong to Changsha, had given me unwelcome experience and was no fun at all. She let the issue drop until I told her one day that Bob, Marcy and Bill were planning a trip to Wuhan to spend a holiday weekend with the Yale-China teachers living there. Actually, I had already decided to join them, but I did not want to rob Teacher Wei of the opportunity to talk me into it. After I promised her that I would go to Wuhan if she really thought I should, she wanted to know who was going to arrange our travel.

"Teacher Wei, it is only a six-hour train ride."

"Yes, but who will buy the tickets for you? Who will see you to the train station? Who will see to it that you get seats?"

"Teacher Wei, we will just take the bus to the station, get in line, buy the tickets, and find seats ourselves."

She could not understand why I would not allow her to get all of her relatives in Changsha and Wuhan to arrange our passage.

"It is my duty to help you!"

"We will be all right, Teacher Wei. It is only for a weekend."

"Well, when will you be back?"

"Monday night."

"Which train will you take?"

"Probably this one—the one that arrives at dinner time."

"I see."

The weekend in Wuhan turned out to be fun, although I did not enjoy the train ride either way. Going up we sat on pieces of newspaper on the floor between two cars, knee to knee with three exhausted men traveling from South to North China. On the way down it was so crowded there was not even room on the floor between cars, so we stood, packed like cattle, with our faces pressed against a mountain of cabbages stacked up to the ceiling of the train. Bob had the clever idea of anchoring his arms in the pile of cabbages and leaning against it so he could sleep, so I followed his example and managed to doze for a few hours. When we got back to Changsha we stopped at a shop for some noodles in broth as the sun went down, before going home.

By the time we reached the gate of our college it was nearly dark. As I passed through it I heard someone calling my name and turned to see Teacher Wei waving at me from under a tree. I walked over and asked if she was on her way somewhere.

"No—I am waiting for you."

"Why are you waiting for me?"

"This was your first trip in China. How shameful it would be if no one greeted you when you came home."

Changsha stayed hot and humid through the early part of November. By then I had developed a painful case of athlete's foot and started looking around for some medicine. None of the local stores carried anything for it, and none of my doctor students was familiar with the symptoms. At last someone acquainted with diseases of the skin had a look at me. He recognized the problem right away, but was unable to treat me. Athlete's foot, he told me, had been declared successfully driven out of China, and therefore could be contracted only if one left the Socialist Motherland or had contact with foreigners. For this reason it was now called "Hong Kong Foot," and no medicine was available for it. He advised me to have someone send medicine from the States.

I wrote someone in Hong Kong and he put a few tubes of medicine, along with some candy bars and brownies, in a small cardboard box and mailed it to me right away.

A few days later a pick-up notice addressed to me showed up in our mailbox. I walked over to the post office and handed it to a young woman behind the counter. She snatched it out of my hand, marched into the back room, came out with my package—torn open, its contents in disarray— dropped it on the counter, slapped a bill in front of me and barked, "Sign and pay!" She seemed to be in terrible humor and refused to look me in the eye, choosing to glare at the clock on the wall instead. I looked at the bill and saw that it imposed on me a tax that surpassed the value of the package's contents.

I took a deep breath and risked all by asking the woman to

explain the tax. Her face turned white and her nostrils flared. "Import tax for Foreign Friends! Hurry up!" I began to get annoyed, because I had been told repeatedly by the Foreign Affairs Bureau that this tax was waived for foreigners living and working in China. It was supposed to be levied only on foreign travelers, who presumably are all rich and don't mind being exploited. When I explained this to the young woman, she yelled, "Then let the Foreign Affairs Bureau pay the tax!" shoved my box to the far side of the counter, and refused to pay attention to me anymore.

I stalked over to the Foreign Affairs Bureau office, calming myself by anticipating the satisfaction of thrusting an official document bristling with angry red seals under that woman's nose. She would have to surrender my box or be sent to a labor camp. But when I told Comrade Hu at the bureau about the problem, instead of giving me an official document he told me not to worry, that the Foreign Affairs Bureau would "research the matter" for me. In Chinese bureaucratic language, "researching a matter" means putting it aside until it solves itself or just goes away, so I pressed him for a better answer. He said he understood the need for expediency and smilingly agreed to "look into the matter," which is usually better than "researching the matter."

A few days later I visited the Foreign Affairs Bureau again to see if my medicine had been released.

"Oh yes," Comrade Hu said, smiling, "it is a very simple problem. You see, this tax is imposed on foreigners who import things into China that China already has. China is a developing country, but nevertheless has medicine and food of its own. For someone to import medicine and food insults our country and the government assumes that foreigners wish to exploit Chinese people by selling foreign goods to them at high prices, saying that their foreign goods are better than

Chinese goods. Of course, we know that you wouldn't do anything like that! You are a friend of China! But, unfortunately, we don't control the regulations!"

"Yes, Comrade Hu, I understand that, but I was told that this import tax applied only to foreigners traveling in China, not to those living and working in China."

After a pause and a few words with Group Leader Chen, Comrade Hu smiled again.

"Yes, exactly. But the Postal Customs officials in Canton get confused. Apparently they don't have your name on their list of foreign residents. So why don't you just pay the tax. We will examine the matter for you, and Canton will reimburse you in no time."

Not wishing to let responsibility for the matter shift to Canton, I tried something else.

"Since this is an internal matter, Comrade Hu, why doesn't your office pay the tax, and then have Canton reimburse you?"

After another pause, and a few more words with Group Leader Chen, Comrade Hu smiled and answered, "Our office, I am sorry to say, is not authorized to disburse funds. If you like, though, we can look into the possibility of having the Health Office of the medical college pay the tax for you. It might take some time for us to determine exactly which channels to go through, however."

Knowing that I had been defeated, I said I would think about it and let them know later. They smiled, and Comrade Hu told me that anytime anything came up I should feel free to come see them. That way, even if we couldn't solve a problem right away, we could come to understand it.

I felt I had had enough of the matter for the time being, and decided to pay the tax the next day. At dinner that night the wife of an American doctor doing research at our hospital mentioned to me that she had a package of mine. She brought it out and indeed it was my medicine and chocolates—she had seen it on the counter at the post office in the afternoon, saw that it was for me, and innocently walked out with it. Our little American community cheered this small victory over the forces of evil, and I went to bed a happy man.

The next day we received no mail. The day after that, we again received no mail. The third day without mail I went to the post office.

I walked straight to the counter where the young woman worked and stood there until finally she hissed, "What do you want?" I answered as quietly as possible that we had not been getting any mail recently, was there a problem? Without looking up she pointed at a pile of mail in the far corner of the room, on her side of the counter—all international mail. I asked if I could pick it up, and once more she slapped the tax bill on the counter. I paid up without a word, and that afternoon we got a big pile of mail.

Several weeks after I had taken my receipt to the Foreign Affairs Bureau, Canton announced that Postal Regulations had changed, and all related debts owed to foreigners had become void.

I spoke some Cantonese and hoped to keep it up while I was in China, since Cantonese is useful in southern China and in most overseas Chinese communities, where people may understand Mandarin but not be able to speak it. The two dialects are so different that, while visiting Guangdong Province where Cantonese is the native language, northern Chinese traveling through the province often asked me to translate for them. There were several Cantonese families living in our *danwei*, or unit, so I passed word around that when they saw me they should speak Cantonese to force me to practice. The Cantonese, who are in general very proud of their language and distinct customs, were all too happy to fulfill my request. One man, a physiology teacher, offered to tutor me regularly in exchange for English lessons. We prepared some materials and agreed to meet once a week for two hours.

Mr. Gong was patient, generous, and extremely polite; I had warm feelings for him, but our friendship was very formal and therefore a bit exhausting. During our conversations I sat up straight in my chair to seem fully attentive, and since he always smiled, I always smiled as well. When he spoke about his experiences during the Second World War and the Cultural Revolution he leaned forward and indicated that I should lean forward too, so that he could whisper into my ear. During these tragic stories he continued to smile, making me self-conscious—it was difficult to maintain an expression of concern or sympathy when he was smiling, yet I could not smile at his misfortune.

He especially liked to tell me about the countryside, where

he had lived for several years when he was "sent down" for ideological reform. Although that was certainly a time of hardship for him, he spoke fondly of the impoverished villagers with whom he had lived and seemed to have great respect for their courage and sincerity. Once, a young boy from a neighboring village ran a high fever. Mr. Gong heard about the boy and went to see if there was anything he could do. He managed to keep the fever under control and the boy recovered, but the boy's father was deeply ashamed that he did not have even a piece of cloth to offer as a token of gratitude.

Thirteen years later this same peasant, having traveled more than one hundred miles on foot and on the backs of trucks, appeared at the gate of Hunan Medical College with three baskets of eggs. When he found Mr. Gong he said, "At last I have something to give you." Then he left, too ashamed of his appearance to visit Mr. Gong's home.

One day Mr. Gong asked me what I liked to do in my spare time. Among other things, I mentioned that I liked taking walks. From that time on he insisted that we have our lessons on foot, and he led me to most of the parks, zoos, museums and monuments in Changsha. These walks lasted two or three hours, and whenever we passed a food stand or restaurant he would treat me to candies, beer or noodles, no matter how I might protest. As good as his intentions were, walking through the noisy streets of Changsha was trying, especially while learning a language. When I suggested that we go back to having lessons in my room, he thought I was only being polite, so I asked instead if we could have our lessons in his home.

I thought I saw him wince, but he agreed right away and assured me that it would be no trouble at all for him or his family. I was to come one evening the next week.

As soon as I entered his home I realized that it had been considerable trouble for him and his family, for not only was the entire three-room apartment spotlessly clean, but a nine-course banquet was waiting for me on the dinner table. My heart sank with guilt, but I made myself register surprise and delight at the elaborate meal that I had virtually forced them to prepare.

Mr. Gong's household consisted of his mother, his wife and his two sons. The older boy was eighteen years old and went to college in the city, and the younger, twelve, was still in middle school. Though they all must have worked for days to get ready for my visit, they seemed genuinely excited that I had come and took great pride in introducing each of the dishes—all Cantonese specialties—to me.

The older son had to leave early to get back to his college, so we all walked him to the bus stop and saw him off. When we got back to the apartment, attention shifted to the younger son, and Mr. Gong asked him to show me his drawing pad. The boy looked embarrassed but obediently produced a sketch pad filled with pencil drawings of Japanese soldiers beheading Chinese peasants. As he handed it to me, I noticed that he wore exceptionally thick glasses.

"My boy is very near-sighted," Mr. Gong said, putting his hand on his son's head. "He will not be able to go to college because he cannot pass the eye examination. We all hope he will learn a trade soon so that his future will not be so uncertain. We keep telling him he must get serious and take responsibility for his future. So far, his only interest seems to be drawing." The boy looked at the ground as his father spoke, then silently retrieved his pad from me and disappeared into the bedroom.

The next day I stopped by Mr. Gong's house to distribute some gifts I had chosen for him and his family that morning.

They were very ordinary gifts, except for the one I gave to the younger son. I had been moved by the story of his interest in drawing and had decided to give him the watercolors, br .shes and charcoals that I had brought from America.

Not long after, Mr. Gong and his son appeared at my door. After a gentle nudge from his father, the trembling boy thanked me for the gift. After another gentle nudge, he asked me with utmost humility if I would be so generous as to teach him to draw. His request was so charming I felt I could not refuse; on the other hand, I did not want to take full responsibility for his career as an artist. I fumbled for words, and at last agreed to come three or four times to show him how to use the materials.

I went to their home that Sunday night after dinner and they had a three-course "snack" waiting. Then the table was cleared and Mr. Gong and his wife reverently placed my watercolors and charcoals on it. Five stools were placed at the table, and the boy sat to my right, with his father, mother and grandmother huddled around him. I thought I would explain how to use the charcoal first, to see if he understood the principles of three-point perspective, before going on to the watercolors. I set a piece of paper in front of him and one in front of me, handed him a charcoal stick, and told him to imitate me. I drew a broad line across the paper using the side of the stick, showing him how to change the width of the line as he liked with his wrist. Nervously he began his line, but he pressed too hard, breaking the delicate stick. His parents and grandmother gasped and quietly scolded him, "Look what you did, you broke it!", and Mr. Gong apologized to me for his son's clumsiness. The boy's face reddened but showed no emotion. I quickly explained that a broken charcoal stick is as useful as a whole one. To put him at ease, I broke my own with a comic gesture and showed him how to use the different-sized pieces to advantage. He did not seem particularly amused, but neither did he seem too upset to go on.

I put a teacup in front of us and suggested that we each try to draw it; that way I could give him some tips as we went along. His every move met with his parents' gentle but firm criticism: "You see the way Uncle Mark did it? Yours doesn't look the same. Imitate Uncle Mark, that's why he has come here." "Why are you making trembly, crooked lines? Concentrate, don't just play—Uncle Mark's time is very precious, don't waste it." I tried to make him feel better by pointing out that trembly, crooked lines can be expressive, and used them to draw a cartoon of a frightened pig to show him what I meant. I thought I saw him smile, but his parents reminded him that I was only being kind, and that he should remember to concentrate next time.

Any American twelve-year-old would have exploded in embarrassment or resentment, but the boy did not protest or even frown. He stoically continued to draw, showing no signs of either exasperation or pleasure.

At last I could bear the gravity no longer, so I leaned back and said to the boy that the most important thing was that he should enjoy learning to draw.

"Are you having fun?" I asked him, praying that he would answer yes.

"Aren't you having fun? Tell him!" his parents said at once, smiling.

"Yes," he replied, with neither irony nor joy.

And then it occurred to me what a burdensome affair this must be for the child, obliged to relieve the anxieties of his parents by displaying sober, concentrated effort, and to please the American, who demanded that he enjoy himself. He met the situation bravely, looking only at the paper and charcoal in front of him—as if the rest of us were too far away to be quite in focus—and maintaining an expression vague enough to allow for interpretation.

A few weeks after I had taught him how to use all the materials, I happened to bump into him walking to the market with his father. I asked about his progress, but he only looked down. His father sighed and patted him on the head.

"Aiya," he sighed, "my foolish boy. He has stopped drawing and seems to have become interested in sports. What will we do with him?"

卷

Peking Duck

Pan

A Fisherman

Kissing

A Suicide

Five minutes after the bell rang for afternoon class, the Middle-Aged English Teachers gradually trickled into the classroom and argued with each other for a few minutes. It seemed that the blackboard had gone unerased the night before, and they were trying to determine who among them had been responsible for erasing it. I saw that the discussion could easily fill the two hours, so I asked them to put it off until after class and to open their textbooks to Chapter Thirteen. That chapter was entitled "War" and contained two pages of photographs of World War II destruction, including a shot of the atomic bomb explosion over Hiroshima.

After they had settled down I had them read passages from the text and do a few grammar exercises. As usual, we finished up with "free talk" on the chapter. Since China and the United States fought on the same side during World War II, I did not think this would be an offensive or controversial subject.

"Teacher Zhu, you were a Navy man, can you tell us something about your experiences during the war?"

Teacher Zhu, an aspiring Party member, stood up and smiled.

"Yes." He hesitated. "This is a picture of the atom bomb, isn't it?"

"Yes."

He smiled stiffly. "Teacher Mark—how do you feel, knowing your country dropped an atom bomb on innocent people?"

My face turned red with embarrassment at having the question put so personally, but I tried to remain detached.

"That is a good question, Teacher Zhu. I can tell you that in America, many people disagree about this. Not everyone thinks it was the right thing to do, although most people think that it saved lives."

"How did it save lives?"

"Well, by ending the war quickly."

Here, Teacher Zhu looked around the room at his classmates.

"But Teacher Mark! It is a fact that the Japanese had already surrendered to the Communist Eighth Route Army of China. America put the bomb on Japan to make the world think America was the . . . the . . ."

"The victor!" shouted Fatty Du.

"Yes—the victor," said Teacher Zhu.

I must have stood gaping for a long time, for the other students began to laugh nervously.

"Teacher Zhu," I asked, "how do you know this is a fact?"

"Because that is what our newspapers say!"

"I see. But our newspapers tell a different story—how can we know which newspaper has told the truth?"

Here he seemed relieved.

"That is easy! Our newspapers are controlled by the people, but your newspapers are owned by capitalist organizations, so of course they make things up to support themselves. Don't you think so?"

My mouth opened and closed a few times but no sound came out. Fatty Du, apparently believing that the truth had been too much for me, came to my aid.

"It doesn't matter! Any capitalist country would do that —it is not just your country!"

My head swimming, I asked her if she thought only capitalist countries lied in the papers.

"Oh, of course not! The Russians do it, too. But here in China we have no reason to lie in the papers. When we make a mistake, we admit it! As for war, there is nothing to lie about—if you look at history, you can see that China has never attacked a nation, it has only defended its borders. We love peace. If we were the most powerful country in the world, think how peaceful the world would be!"

I said that I certainly agreed that war was a terrible thing and that I was glad that China and the United States had become so friendly. The class applauded my speech and said that things were much better now that America was their friend than when Russia was their friend.

After our ten-minute break for tea between the two hours, I decided to put away the textbook and ask them to read aloud their latest compositions, entitled "My Happiest Moment." They all thought this was a very good idea, but no one wanted to read first. Finally I called on Teacher Xu. He shrugged his shoulders with resignation and began.

"My happiest moment. When I was a young man I attended a dance at night. We were all very excited about this dance. The music was being played, and stars shone brightly. I saw a girl standing, and wanted to ask her to dance, but as I am shy and full of fear I did not dare! But then I did, and we danced. I did not know her name. We did not talk, we only danced. We danced in circles, around and around, and the stars went around and around, and my cheek touched hers.

The room disappeared, the other people disappeared, and I could only see the stars dancing around and around. After that, I did not see her ever again. I wonder where she is."

The rest of the class clicked their tongues in mock disapproval of his romantic story and teased him, asking if he had shown this essay to his wife. Teacher Xu smiled faintly, shrugged again and said, "She cannot read English."

I called on Teacher Cai, famed in our college for his beautiful wife, to read next.

"In the 1950's, many Russians come to our country. These are so-called advisors. How terrible it was! They were not friendly as Americans, dear Teacher Mark. No! They drove in large, black cars and would not be friends of common people like us. They were not happy to be in China, I think. They held big dances, drank vodka and danced with our Chinese girls, and often tried to kiss them! We hated the advisors very much, but at that time we cannot say this, we can only be silent."

Everyone began to speak at once, confirming this account, but Teacher Cai said "Shhhh!" and continued. "One day there was a wonderful news—I was helping my wife to cooking then—the Leaders of our country told the Russian hegemonists to go home. When I heard this, I am sure this was my happiest moment."

Fatty Du, beaming in memory of the Russians' expulsion, volunteered to go next.

"Although I live in Changsha, I did not always live here. I was born in the eastern part of our country, in a little village. During the war our life was terrible. We often had to run into the mountains to escape the Japanese soldiers. Many times our village was destroyed, and we were always filled with sorrow in our hearts. After 1945, the life of our village did not improve much. Everyone was very poor and the government of the Kuomintang was not helping the people. All of us felt hopeless. Then we began to hear about the liberation of villages by the Communists, and we were full of hope. When the Communists came and liberated our village, I remember our village welcoming the soldiers. How proud and strongly they were! How gay and joyous we were! I remember that we found everything red in color, even pieces of paper, and held them in our hands to wave as the soldiers marched. Around my neck I wore a red piece of cloth. This was my happiest moment."

Next I called on Teacher Zhang, known for his fear of Fatty Du. At first he declined to read; sitting sideways in his chair and shaking his head, he said he was a sad man and could not remember a happy moment. But his colleagues insisted that he had written an essay and coaxed him into reading it aloud.

"I love my parents and my brothers and sisters very much. I think of them every day. After I graduated from college I felt proudly and my family was happy for me. But then I received the news: I was assigned to Hunan Medical College. I am from Beijing, far away from here. Beijing is a wonderful place and Hunan is a terrible place. The weather and general situation is terrible.

"I tried to convince the Leaders to change it so I could stay with my family but it was impossible, and I must go where the Party sends me. When I got on the train, I did not know when I could come back again, and I cried for a thousand miles.

"Several years later our college gave me permission to visit my family. When the train arrived in Beijing, my whole family was at the station to meet me. I had so much to tell them, I had planned on the whole train ride all the stories I would tell them, but when I saw them, no words came out from my mouth. I only stood there and tears fell out of my eyes like rain. This was my happiest moment."

Teacher Zhu read last.

"My story is very common, because I am a very common man. In the winter of 1975 I traveled to Beijing. My relative in Beijing invited me to a restaurant famous for its Beijing duck. On a cold day we walked in the restaurant. Inside was warm and comfortable! We sat down and the banquet started. First we ate cold dishes, such as marinated pig stomach and sea slugs. Then we had steamed fish, then at last the duck arrived! The skin was brown and crisp and shiny, in my mouth it was like clouds disappearing. The sauces were various and delicious, and each piece of skin we put in a *bing* —Teacher Mark, how do you say *bing* in English?"

"We call them pancakes."

"Pancakes. Each piece of skin we put in a 'pancakes' with sauce and scallions. Afterwards we had the duck meat with vegetables. After that we had duck bone soup and fruits."

He seemed to be finished, but then he put his composition down and smiled sheepishly at me.

"Teacher Mark. I have to tell you something. Actually this story is true, but actually I have never been to Beijing. Can you guess? My wife went to Beijing and had this duck. But she often tells me about it again and again, and I think, even though I was not there, it is my happiest moment."

Early one Saturday morning in March one of my doctor students knocked at my door. A cold, steady drizzle that had been falling since January had convinced me to stay in bed as long as possible, but at ten past seven a terrific pounding and the voice of Dr. Nie calling my name woke me from a dream. I remember the dream clearly. A team of cadres from the Public Security Bureau had tied me by my feet to a giant ferris wheel, so that each time it completed a circle my head scraped along the ground. Once awake, I thought I might keep silent and pretend to be out, as I was in no mood to smile and answer grammar questions at that hour. Then I heard Old Sheep telling Dr. Nie that I hadn't gotten up yet, so he should just knock louder. When the pounding became unbearable I got up. I didn't bother putting clothes on over my several layers of woolen underwear, and tried to look as much like hell as I could manage, but this only seemed to amuse him. "Follow me," he said, and started down the stairs. My annoyance grew as he yelled from the front door for me to hurry. I told him that I had something to do. That was all right, he didn't mind, and he laughed— let's go! I said I was expecting a visitor any minute now, so I couldn't leave the house; he said it didn't matter, and laughed—let's go! I said I didn't feel well, maybe we could go out and play another day; he said we could do that, too, and laughed—hurry up! I put on some clothes, went downstairs and pleaded with him to leave me alone, but he grabbed my arm and pulled me out of the house. "Do you have grammar questions this morning, Dr. Nie?" I asked. "Thank you," he answered, and led me out of the college gate.

I was in a poor mood as we wandered through the streets, splashing up coal dust mixed with rain, at seven-fifteen in the morning. I could only hope that this would be a half-day outing instead of the full-day English-speaking marathons our students loved so well. At least it was winter; if it had been warmer out, I would have been obliged to spend several hours in a rented rowboat at Martyrs' Park eating dried melon seeds and enjoying "free talk" with no hope of inter-ruption or distraction. "Free talk" involved relentless, vigor-ous conversation of absolutely no import that drove me to near-madness. Floating helplessly in the middle of a dirty pond only made it worse. "Where are we going?" I asked. "A surprise," he answered, and I shuddered to imagine what it could be.

Twenty minutes later we came to the gate of the Provincial Sports Unit, a large complex for the Hunan athletes. Each province in China has such a unit, where the best athletes live and train. They receive their education there, too, but an abbreviated one. They are the closest thing to professional athletes China has, and they spend most of their time training.

I remembered that Dr. Nie specialized in athletic medicine and performed surgery on the more serious cases that arose in this unit. He led me to a large five-story cement building, which had a training space on its uppermost floor, judging from the arrangement of its windows. We climbed the filthy, unlit staircase and Dr. Nie paused in front of two large wooden doors to savor the moment. He turned and smiled at me, indicating that I should listen. I heard through the doors a cacophony of cracks, whooshes and thuds. Just as it began to dawn on me what might be going on, he swung open the doors to reveal a dingy, cavernous room with bare cement walls and a dull red carpet on the floor.

Ten or eleven young men and women in battered sweat-suits stood around against the walls, watching silently as three of their colleagues engaged in furious armed combat. Two of the men had six-foot wooden poles, and were teamed up to defeat the third, who wielded a three-section staff—three short poles connected by chains. Even in the movies, with the assistance of trick photography and trampolines, I had never seen anything to match this fight. I felt my stomach tighten, thinking one of the fighters would surely be brained by the poles, which swung by so fast I could barely see them. Suddenly, in perfect unison, the two with the long poles froze in position, poised for the last attack. The other athletes tensed, and all was quiet for a full second. Then several of them shrieked, and the fighters seemed to go mad, rushing into their final clash. The man with the three-section staff leapt into the air, rolled over the back of one of his opponents, and took an overhead swing at them both. They moved out of the way just in time and the weapon crashed to the ground, inches from their feet, with such force that the whole carpet shook and the air filled with dust. Without stopping, the three spun and froze again in an atti-tude of readiness, held it, then doubled over to breathe. The assistant trainer, a frail-looking woman in her thirties, walked over to them and barked a few words of criticism on the routine, then told them to get out of the way for the next group. The three fighters, who looked more like panthers than humans, loped off to one side. Immediately, two young women marched to the center of the room. Theirs was to be an unarmed battle.

They stood about an arm's length from one another, staring straight ahead. The trainer gave a yell and the two women turned their heads to exchange a deadly glance before exploding into action. One of the women was fairly tall, with long hair put up in a bun; the other was short, with thick shoulder-length hair that hung loose around her face. The tall woman began the attack, lashing out with a back-fist. The short woman leaned back so that it just grazed her throat, spinning around and jumping into the air as she did so, so that her right leg swung in an arc that ended full-force on the chest of the tall woman. Both crashed to the ground and lay still. Then, as if they had springs underneath them, they bounced up into the air and continued to fight. What struck me most about these women was their power; they hit with enough force to knock a large man unconscious. The short woman, especially, fought like a demon. I found out later that she had doubled for the heroines in the fight scenes of several movies. But she was not to be the main attraction this morning. After the women finished up, Dr. Nie led me into the room. The men looked at me curiously. The women all giggled and shifted to the far corner of the room, taking turns looking quickly at me and then at the ground.

The assistant trainer came over to greet us. Dr. Nie introduced her as Little Liu, and me as the American Professor Mr. Sima Ming (my Chinese name). I had to go through this ritual at least once a day in China, where "distinguished Foreign Guests" must be introduced politely, meaning that their credentials are blown well out of proportion. I explained to her that I was not a professor, but an English teacher, and that since she was older than me, she should refer to me as Little Sima, but she and Dr. Nie agreed that since I had been educated in America, I should be a professor, and that since I had traveled far, my experience was great, so I should at least be Mr. Sima Ming.

Little Liu pointed to the athletes. "These are the members of the Hunan Provincial Wushu Troupe. Today you are our guest. Please feel free to ask any questions you like, and voice your criticisms to help us improve." "Where is he?" Dr. Nie asked her. "He'll come soon," she assured him, "but he didn't want to get here first. He wanted the professor to wait a while." Liu invited me to sit down on one of the long wooden benches that lined the walls of the room. "Now they'll practice their solo routines."

The solo routines of wushu are something like floor exercises in gymnastics; each routine is a prearranged series of moves, created by the master and student together, that best displays the student's versatility and special strengths, but within the aesthetic boundaries of that particular style of wushu. For example, a double-edged sword routine must not contain moves characteristic of sabre. Each style has its own repertoire and personality, and mixing them is considered a sign of poor taste or careless training.

First, one of the young men who had been fighting earlier with a long pole performed the "Drunken Sword." In this style the fighter must stumble, weave, leap and bob as if drunk, at the same time whipping his sword around him at full speed, all the while maintaining perfect control. Then a woman with a single braid reaching to her waist performed the double sabre. The two blades flashed around her but never touched, and she finished by leaping into the air, crossing the sabres and landing in a full split. One after the other, the athletes performed routines with spears, halberds, hooks, knives and their bare hands. My stomach hurt by now just from the excitement of watching them; I'd never seen martial arts of this quality before, nor sat so close to such tremendous athletes as they worked. Just as the last man finished a routine with the nine-section steel whip, someone clapped once, and all the athletes rushed into a line and stood at perfect attention. I turned toward the wooden doors to see who had clapped and for the first time saw Pan.

I recognized him immediately as one of the evil characters in *Shaolin Temple,* and I knew from magazine articles about the movie that he had choreographed and directed the martial arts scenes. This movie, shot partly on location at the real Shaolin temple where Chinese boxing has been practiced for more than fifteen hundred years, featured China's most famous boxers and was produced and distributed by studios in Hong Kong. It became an immediate success in East Asia when it was released in 1981, and remains China's only block-buster film to date. Not long after my arrival in Changsha, several people had mentioned to me that someone connected with this movie was in Hunan, but no one had actually seen him or could agree upon who he was. They did agree, how-ever, that one would need a significant "back door" to gain an introduction, if he was really in Hunan at all. Pan had a massive reputation as a fighter from the days when scores were settled with blows rather than points. His nickname, "Iron Fist," was said to describe both his personality and his right hand, which he had developed by punching a fifty-pound iron plate nailed to a concrete wall one thousand to ten thousand times a day.

Pan walked over to where the athletes stood, looked them over, and told them to relax. They formed a half-circle around him; some leaned on one leg or crossed their arms, but most remained at stiff attention. He gave them his morn-ing address in a voice too low for me to hear, but it was clear from the expressions on his face that he was exhorting them to push harder, always harder, otherwise where will you get?

He stood about five foot eight, with a medium to slight build, a deep receding hairline, a broad, scarred nose and upper front teeth so badly arranged that it looked as if he had two rows of them, so that if he bit you and wrecked the first set, the second would grow in to replace them. Most noticeable, though, were his eyebrows. They swept up toward his temples making him look permanently angry, as if he were wearing some sort of Peking Opera mask. At one point he gestured to one of the athletes with his right hand, and I saw that it was strangely disfigured. Dr. Nie, who must have known what I was thinking, leaned over and said, "That is the iron fist."

Pan looked fearsome, but what most distinguished him was that, when he talked, his face moved and changed expression. I had been in China for eight months, but thought this was the first time I had seen a Chinese person whose face moved. Sometimes his eyes opened wide with surprise, then narrowed with anger, or his mouth trembled with fear and everyone laughed, then he ground his teeth and looked ready to avenge a murder. His eyebrows, especially, were so mobile that I wondered if they had been knocked loose in one of his brawls. He commanded such presence that, for the duration of his address, no one seemed to breathe.

At last he finished. He clapped his hands once again and the athletes jumped back to their positions in the room, ready to continue their morning workout. He started to walk toward the far side of the room, where all the weapons lay on a wooden rack, then pretended to notice us for the first time. He looked surprised, spread his palms in a welcoming gesture, then said to Dr. Nie, "Why didn't you tell me we had a guest?"

Dr. Nie introduced me once again as Professor Mr. Sima Ming, this time adding that I was a wushu expert and had performed several times in China with great success. "The professor practiced Chinese martial arts for nine years before coming to China and has performed not only for our college, but for the governor of Hunan as well." While this was true, it was not true that I was an expert, or that the success of my performances was due to the quality of my wushu. Anything a foreigner did in front of a Chinese audience received thunderous applause. "He is especially good at 'Drunken Fist'." In fact, I knew very little Drunken Fist, but since all my performances occurred after huge banquets, where drinking contests with baijiu were required, my thrashing about was usually identified as "Drunken Fist." I would typically jump over a table, trip over a chair and throw it around, fall down a few times, punch an imaginary opponent and leave to be sick. Before I could explain all this, though, Dr. Nie turned to our host and said, "And this is Master Pan Qingfu. There is no need to introduce him further."

Pan extended his hand for me to shake. It was not deformed, but simply decorated with several large calluses on his knuckles and finger joints that had turned black as if scorched. I put my hand in his, and to my great surprise and relief, he shook it gently. We sat down and he asked how it happened that I spoke Chinese and lived in China.

As we spoke the troupe continued to practice, even more furiously than before, now that Pan had arrived. Every few minutes he pointed to his stopwatch, shook his head and asked some poor athlete if he was napping or practicing. He criticized one of the women so fiercely that it looked as if she were on the verge of tears. He made her repeat a move, a complicated leap ending in a crouched position, until she collapsed in a heap on the floor. "Who's next?" he shouted, and another athlete came forward, taking care not to step on the woman as she dragged herself off to the side. None of the athletes even twitched an eyebrow when receiving instructions or criticism. He ordered, and instantly they obeyed, without so much as a sigh, and they obeyed in this fashion until they could no longer stand.

After two hours or so morning practice came to an end. Pan reminded them to be on time for afternoon practice and seemed about to dismiss them when a smile came over his face. He pointed at me. "Please welcome our American friend." The athletes burst into applause, smiling with what energy they had left. "He has practiced wushu for nine years —don't you think he should do something for us?" The applause turned to cheers of delight. I felt all the blood drain from my face and thought I would faint if I stood up. As soon as I could speak I refused, but this only brought louder cheering. Dr. Nie, ever the friend in need, announced that I was just being modest, and that I was as strong as a lion and fast as a swooping pigeon, or something like that, and began to pull me from the bench. I looked at Pan; he was smiling at me the way a wolf might smile at a lame deer.

Then the blood rushed back into my face, and I nearly saw double with anger. Humiliating unwitting foreigners is something of a popular sport in China, and it occurred to me that my little spectacle would soon be legendary. But he had me. If I accepted, I would go down in local history as the foreigner who made a fool of himself in front of Pan Qingfu and the Hunan Wushu Troupe; if I refused, I would be remembered as the foreigner who left the Hunan Sports Unit with his tail between his legs.

I stood up, and the applause died down. Pan sat down, continuing to smile. I explained that my wushu couldn't be compared to theirs and added, truthfully, that I had never imagined I would see such expertise as they possessed. I then said that for me to perform a Chinese routine would be a waste of time, since they did wushu so much better. I had come to learn. Better for me to do something they might not otherwise have a chance to see. I told them that in America, fighters have been exposed to a variety of Asian martial arts, Western boxing, and African dancing rhythms. Making it up as I went along, I explained that a distinctly American style has come out of all this, and is called "On the Street Boxing." I started clapping out a syncopated beat, began moving in a modified hustle, and let loose, trying to make up for what I lacked in gymnastic skill with unrestrained violence. At the time I was not in good condition, so after a few minutes, when I started to taste blood in my throat, I stopped. The athletes exploded into cheers, and Dr. Nie slapped Pan's shoulders in excitement, but Pan sat dead still, with the same smile on his face. I started to see black around the edges of my field of vision and no longer heard all the noise, but only saw Pan at the end of a darkening tunnel. He stood up and walked toward me, stopping when his face was very near my own. His smile had disappeared. In a very low voice he said, "That's not gong fu." We stared at each other for a long time, then he raised one eyebrow. "I could fix it, if you wanted." I must have nodded, because then he asked me if I could *chi ku*, eat bitter, the Chinese expression meaning to endure suffering. Lying, I said yes. Then he asked me if I was afraid of pain. Lying again, I said no. "You want?" he asked. "I want," I said, and became his student.

Early one morning a heavy fog fell over the city. Right away I thought of going down to the river to see what it looked like. I put a few pieces of steamed bread into a small covered pot, got on my bicycle and rode down to the end of Anti-Imperialism Road. I parked the bicycle against a tree, went down the stone steps of the flood wall to the riverbank and sat on a discarded tire.

I hoped that I might see the fog rise, or at least have the sun burst through an opening and light it all up, but nothing like that happened. I ate my steamed bread and was getting ready to leave when something caught my eye. Out of the fog slipped a tiny boat with a fisherman standing in it, rowing slowly and singing to himself. Chinese rowboats, unchanged for many centuries, are shaped like cigars and have a curved roof of woven bamboo at one end. The oars are longer than Western oars, crossing in front of the oarsman to form an X. The oarsman stands at the rear of the boat, facing forward, with the oars in front of him. He pushes them through the water, pulling them for the return stroke. The fisherman stopped not far from me and took out his net, which was folded neatly into a ball and had several round metal weights dangling from it. He walked to the front of the boat, got his footing, wound up and threw the net. It spun in the air, and the weights went their separate directions, opening the round net like a flower before it hit the surface of the water and disappeared. After waiting a few minutes he pulled it in, taking a few wriggling fish out and dropping them into a bucket. He folded the net carefully and prepared to move on. Just as he took the oars in his hands, he saw me.

I cannot imagine what goes through a Chinese fisherman's or peasant's mind when he sees a white man for the first time, but I can describe the physical reaction: paralysis, and the mouth drops open. This is what happened that morning, and only when the current started to spin his boat around did he come to and start rowing. He rowed slowly past me, his mouth still open, close enough that I could see that he was barefoot, in the winter, and that his hands were dark and swollen from all the time they spent in the cold water. I smiled at him and he beamed back, waving so vigorously he nearly fell out of the boat. I said hello and asked him if he wasn't cold without shoes on, and he dropped both oars, clapping his hands with delight. It was obvious that he simply could not believe that I spoke Chinese. He picked up the oars, rowed frantically over to where I stood and stretched out his hand to help me into the boat. "Jump on!" he yelled, "I have to show you to my family!" At first I hesitated, but then I remembered that I was not in New Haven anymore and would probably not be mugged, so I took his hand and got on.

We rowed downstream for about half an hour, talking the whole way, though he often had to say things a few times for me to understand him. He tried to speak Mandarin for my benefit, but his Changsha accent made it almost incomprehensible. He seemed most interested in hearing songs from my country. I sang a few lines of this and that as he rowed and asked him if he liked them. "They're not bad, but not as good as Hunan folk songs!" "Would you sing one for me?" "Of course!" I leaned back in the boat and put my arms behind my head while he sang. His broken voice was the perfect instrument for the exquisitely frail melodies, and certainly I could not have heard them under better circumstances.

He stopped singing to point something out to me. Near the river bank, not far ahead, a cluster of five or six boats like his floated together, connected by ropes. "My family!" he said, then urged me to crawl under the bamboo roof. "Don't come out until I tell you!" He rowed up to the flotilla, tied his boat to one of the others and exchanged a few words with someone before winking at me and telling me to come out. I crawled out and stood up. Ten or eleven men and women, young and old, sat together around a portable charcoal stove eating a mid-morning snack. One by one they looked up, and I could see the paralysis hit like a wave until it reached the youngest child, not more than three years old, who burst into tears. My friend doubled over with laughter, and as soon as he could speak he blurted out, "There's more—he talks!" This time I hit them with the smile and the speech all at once, and the effect was stupendous. Before I knew it, I had more food than I could eat in a week set in front of me, the men crowding around me shaking my hands and slapping my shoulders with joy, the women asking me questions all at the same time, and the children fighting to get in line to touch me.

My friend, who called himself Old Ding, was the only one among them able to approximate the sounds of Mandarin, so I couldn't understand a word anyone was saying. I smiled a great deal, though, and that was enough. I became their new friend, and they indicated with sincerity that what was theirs was now also mine. That morning I learned to row their boats, cast a "flower net," as they called it, and set up the larger nets that are pulled shut by two, three, or sometimes six boats.

Around noon I reminded Old Ding that I had a two-thirty

class, so I should be getting back. He, one of his brothers and I hopped into the smallest boat, and after I had said goodbye to the family and promised to return, we started upstream. The Xiang River runs fast, so even with the brothers taking turns rowing vigorously, it took us an hour and a half to get back to the city limits, where my bicycle was parked. The brother had a huge barrel chest, a scarred face and a moustache that made me think of Fu Manchu. He didn't speak so much as growl, or so it seemed to me, and every once in a while he leaned forward to slap me on the shoulder, nearly propelling me out of the boat. He smiled at me, gnashed his teeth and growled. "What is he saying?" I asked Old Ding. "He says he likes you and wants to wrestle! My brother likes to wrestle!"

Before letting me ashore, they insisted that we have one more adventure. A big river boat was anchored in the middle of the river, dredging up silt from the riverbed and dropping it onto flat tugboats that carried it to shore. Old Ding knew the crew and suggested that we stop by and say hello. We rowed alongside the boat and got on quietly. None of the crew saw us, for they were all in the cabin relaxing during xiuxi. The three of us walked into the cabin, me last of all. The captain was the first to look up. He opened his mouth but was unable to speak, and his cigarette fell from his lower lip into his bowl of rice, where it sizzled loudly. Once the initial shock and frenzy died down, the captain gave me a tour of his boat. He told me that he remembered the American soldiers from the Second World War very well. With great emotion in his voice, he repeated over and over how good it was of them to help China. At last, he managed to say "USA!" in English, and gave me the thumbs-up sign.

Eventually we left the river boat and the brothers took me to where I had first gotten on. Only after I agreed to accept the two biggest fish in the hold did they let me ashore. They stood in the boat waving for as long as I could see them, yelling after me that I should come back soon to play, that all I had to do was walk by the river and I would find them. To avoid arriving late for class, I rode directly to the class-room, where I had a difficult time explaining to my doctor students how I came to possess two giant fish that still breathed when I set them on my desk. Every few minutes, just as the curious whispering had died down and we began to go over the lesson, one of the fish would leap into the air and land with a loud slap on the floor. On my way home, I gave the fish to Teacher Wei and told her of my day with the fisherman. She nodded slowly as I told it, and when I had finished, she smiled. "The fishing people are very honest, and very kind. You see how well they treat you? That is the Chinese way. They are common people, but they understand manners better than we intellectuals, who are now cautious and tired."

Two hours later she walked into my room with a covered pot and put it on my desk. It contained one of the fish, cooked to perfection in a spicy Hunan sauce. "Of course," she said as she hurried out, "we intellectuals can still do a pretty good job."

It started with an argument about Nastassia Kinski's lips. *Tess of the D'Urbervilles* was playing in Changsha, and I asked the small group of doctors and teachers from my class what they thought of it. We had just finished an outstanding meal cooked by two of the doctors, husband and wife, and were now relaxing in their small apartment, drinking tea and trying to digest seventeen dishes shared among eight people. The doctors beat around the bush for a while, calling the movie "interesting" and "full of characters," but eventually confessed that they had not enjoyed it much. Among the disappointments of this movie, they said, was that Miss Kinski, the star, was not beautiful. "You can't be serious," I said. but they were, and their complaint was specific: her lips were too big. "They aren't big," I said, "they are full." "Then they are too full," they replied. According to Chinese taste, a woman's lips should be small and delicate. I told them that Westerners consider full lips to be very good, and they asked, "Good for what?"

Middle-aged Chinese intellectuals, I found, do not talk about kissing much. If an American raises the subject, though, it becomes a matter of cultural exchange, and can be discussed in the name of international cooperation. "For kissing," I said. They all exploded into laughter and decided aloud that I was a "very, very naughty boy." They seemed in a fine mood for cultural exchange, so I mentioned that, since coming to China, I had never seen two people kiss each other, even in the movies, except for mothers kissing their infant children. Their eyes opened wide and they nodded vigorously. "Of course not! Here in China, it is very different from your country. People don't kiss here." This I found hard to believe, and asked them if they meant not at all, or just in public. Here lay the boundary of cultural exchange, for suddenly there was an embarrassed spell of throat-clearing and teacup refilling. I didn't want the conversation to turn back to "Can you tell us the secret of learning English?" so I groped for safer material. "What about parents? Do they kiss their children after they grow up?" One or two of the doctors said no, only when they are infants. You shouldn't kiss children after they are two or three years old. And there ended our discussion, for the Small Group Leader of the class, a Party member, pulled out a grammar textbook and began pointing out contradictions.

By ten o'clock most of the guests had gone home, leaving only the hosts, myself and Teacher Liu. I thought it odd that Teacher Liu remained, for of all the students in that class, he was the most shy and the most self-conscious about speaking English. He wrote fairly well, but I had probably heard his voice only three or four times all semester, and he hadn't said anything that night but had sat quietly and looked downward the whole time. He seemed such a gentle man, with greying hair and a reddish glow to his nose after drinking a thimbleful of baijiu; I wanted to speak with him now that the more aggressive talkers had left. He declined to answer my questions, though, looking even further downward, smiling and waving his hand—he was ashamed of his English. Then the husband and wife excused themselves to start cleaning up in the kitchen, but invited us to stay as long as we liked to finish our tea. I waited for Teacher Liu's cue to leave, but he didn't move. The doctors left the room, and I could see that Teacher Liu was thinking about something and trying to form the words silently. I said in Chinese that he could speak Chinese now, the English party was over, but he gestured for me to be patient. Then, very slowly, and with great precision, he said, "Teacher Mark. Do you remember? We said that we do not kiss our children after they are big. You are an honest, and you are my teacher. So I must be an honest, your student. As to kissing, this is not always true. I have two daughters. One is twelve and one is ten. I cannot kiss them, because they would feel embarrassment and they would call me a foolish. But every night, after they are asleep, I go into their room to turn off the light. In fact, very quiet, very soft, I kiss them and they don't know."

Old Sheep's responsibilities gave her, in addition to the keys to our rooms, daily opportunities to get to know us better. In the mornings, when she came in to dust and fill my thermos with hot water, she created such a flurry of movement and noise that I inevitably found myself drawn out of my work and into conversation with her. She always wore a white surgical cap pulled halfway down over her eyes, her strong teeth bared in a huge smile, and carried several tin buckets that crashed together as she walked. She would explode through my door and into the room, greet me in Mandarin —"Ni hao!"—prolonging each syllable for several seconds with her voicebox turned up all the way, wait for my response, then laugh in whoops. With that out of her system, she usually asked me what I had eaten for breakfast, told me it was not nearly enough and that I worked too hard, then related the latest gossip.

Naturally I was curious when one day she entered my room quietly, said "Ni hao" in a subdued voice and did not laugh when I answered. I asked her if something was wrong, and she walked over to where I was sitting so that she could whisper.

"Suicide," she said.

"Who?"

"A woman in our college—a few buildings away. They found her just now."

She began to dust very quickly. Without looking at me, she said, " I want to finish all of my work early today so that I don't have to be out when it gets dark."

"Why not?"

She looked a bit embarrassed and covered her mouth with her hand. "I'm afraid of ghosts. I'm not supposed to believe in ghosts, but I'm afraid of them anyway. The ghost of a suicide wanders around at night."

News travels fast in China, for when I got to the classroom at half past eight, all the doctors were in a huddle, whispering tensely. I asked for the details, but all I could learn was that the woman, a middle-aged clerical worker, had hanged herself in the office of her superior. After class one of the doctors stayed behind to erase the blackboard. I asked if he had any idea why the woman had taken her own life. He looked around and said quietly that he could not be sure, of course, but the rumor was that her superior had been mistreating her for many years. She had complained, but no one wanted to take responsibility for the investigation, so at last she killed herself in despair.

"Do you think it is true?" I asked.

"No one knows what really happened."

"But do you think it is true?"

He paused, then answered, "Maybe."

"What will happen to the superior if the rumor is true?"

A slight frown passed over his face. "He is a Party Member. Anyway, that is not the important thing."

"What is the important thing?"

He looked at me strangely, as if the answer should have been obvious. "The important thing is, what will happen to her family now?"

I did not understand. Patiently he explained to me that, according to Chinese law, most suicides are considered criminal offenses against Socialism and the Communist Party. When someone takes his own life, members of his family are often punished, on the principle that they must have either condoned or been influenced by the "incorrect thought" that led to the suicide. My student predicted that the woman's children would lose their chances of receiving work assignments in our unit when they came of age—a grave sentence, as it would be very difficult for them to get jobs in other units, which have their own surplus of young people to provide jobs for.

Four days passed, during which the woman's family was not allowed to hold any kind of memorial service, and, I was told, few dared visit the family to offer condolences. No one talked about her in my classes, though it was clear she was on everyone's mind.

On the fifth day a poster went up at the gate of our college. The Leaders had announced their decision: "Although Comrade M's suicide was the wrong course of action to take, it was not a crime against Socialism or the Chinese Communist Party because she left no note blaming the Party or any of its representatives for her despair, indicating that her problems were personal and not political. A thorough investigation of the case has proven that her superior, Manager L, is competent and totally without blame. Comrade M's gesture of hanging herself in the office of Manager L was the result of misunderstanding on her part."

A memorial service was held right away, and the woman's house was crowded with friends and neighbors who came to help with the cooking and cleaning. For several days afterward my students talked fondly about her in class, for she had been very popular during her lifetime, and everyone agreed how tragic it was that she had had this misunderstanding.

豆

Lessons

A Garden

A Short Story

"Mei Banfa"

A Ghost Story

I was to meet Pan at the training hall four nights a week, to receive private instruction after the athletes finished their evening work out. Waving and wishing me good night, they politely filed out and closed the wooden doors, leaving Pan and me alone in the room. First he explained that I must start from scratch. He meant it, too, for beginning that night, and for many nights thereafter, I learned how to stand at attention. He stood inches away from me and screamed, "Stand straight!" then bored into me with his terrifying gaze. He insisted that I maintain eye contact for as long as he stood in front of me, and that I meet his gaze with one of equal intensity. After as long as a minute of this silent torture, he would shout "At ease!" and I could relax a bit, but not smile or take my eyes away from his. We repeated this exercise countless times, and I was expected to practice it four to six hours a day. At the time, I wondered what those staring contests had to do with wushu, but I came to realize that everything he was to teach me later was really contained in those first few weeks when we stared at each other. His art drew strength from his eyes; this was his way of passing it on.

After several weeks I came to enjoy staring at him. I would break into a sweat and feel a kind of heat rushing up through the floor into my legs and up into my brain. He told me that when standing like that, I must at all times be prepared to duel, that at any moment he might attack, and I should be ready to defend myself. It exhilarated me to face off with him, to feel his power and taste the fear and anticipation of the blow. Days and weeks passed, but the blow did not come.

One night he broke the lesson off early, telling me that tonight was special. I followed him out of the training hall, and we bicycled a short distance to his apartment. He lived with his wife and two sons on the fifth floor of a large, anonymous cement building. Like all the urban housing going up in China today, the building was indistinguishable from its neighbors, mercilessly practical and depressing in appearance. Pan's apartment had three rooms and a small kitchen. A private bathroom and painted, as opposed to raw, cement walls in all the rooms identified it as the home of an important family. The only decoration in the apartment consisted of some silk banners, awards and photographs from Pan's years as the national wushu champion and from the set of *Shaolin Temple*. Pan's wife, a doctor, greeted me with all sorts of homemade snacks and sat me down at a table set for two. Pan sat across from me and poured two glasses of baijiu. He called to his sons, both in their teens, and they appeared from the bedroom instantly. They stood in complete silence until Pan asked them to greet me, which they did, very politely, but so softly I could barely hear them. They were handsome boys, and the elder, at about fourteen, was taller than me and had a moustache. I tried asking them questions to put them at ease, but they answered only by nodding. They apparently had no idea how to behave toward something like me and did not want to make any mistakes in front of their father. Pan told them to say good night, and they, along with his wife, disappeared into the bedroom. Pan raised his glass and proposed that the evening begin.

He told me stories that made my hair stand on end, with such gusto that I though the building would shake apart. When he came to the parts where he vanquished his enemies, he brought his terrible hand down on the table or against the wall with a crash, sending our snacks jumping out of their serving bowls. His imitations of cowards and bullies were so funny I could hardly breathe for laughing. He had me spellbound for three solid hours; then his wife came in to see if we needed any more food or baijiu. I took the opportunity to ask her if she had ever been afraid for her husband's safety when, for example, he went off alone to bust up a gang of hoodlums in Shenyang. She laughed and touched his right hand. "Sometimes I figured he'd be late for dinner." A look of tremendous satisfaction came over Pan's face, and he got up to use the bathroom. She sat down in his chair and looked at me. "Every day he receives tens of letters from all over China, all from people asking to become his student. Since he made the movie, its been almost impossible for him to go out during the day." She refilled our cups, then looked at me again. "He has trained professionals for more than twenty-five years now, but in all that time he has accepted only one private student." After a long pause, she gestured at me with her chin. "You." Just then Pan came back into the room, returned to his seat and started a new story. This one was about a spear:

While still a young man training for the national wushu competition, Pan overheard a debate among some of his fellow athletes about the credibility of an old story. The story described a famous warrior as being able to execute a thousand spear-thrusts without stopping to rest. Some of the athletes felt this to be impossible: after fifty, one's shoulders ache, and by one hundred the skin on the left hand, which guides the spear as the right hand thrusts, twists and returns it, begins to blister. Pan had argued that surely this particular warrior would not have been intimidated by aching shoulders and blisters, and soon a challenge was raised. The next day Pan went out into a field with a spear, and as the other athletes watched, executed one thousand and seven thrusts without stopping to rest. Certain details of the story as Pan told it—that the bones of his left hand were exposed, and so forth—might be called into question, but the number of thrusts I am sure is accurate, and the scar tissue on his left palm indicates that it was not easy for him.

One evening later in the year, when I felt discouraged with my progress in a form of Northern Shaolin boxing called "Changquan," or "Long Fist," I asked Pan if he thought I should discontinue the training. He frowned, the only time he ever seemed genuinely angry with me, and said quietly, "When I say I will do something, I do it, exactly as I said I would. In my whole life, I have never started something without finishing it. I said that in the time we have, I would make your wushu better than you could imagine, and I will. Your only responsibility to me is to practice and to learn. My responsibility to you is much greater! Every time you think your task is great, think how much greater mine is. Just keep this in mind: if you fail"—here he paused to make sure I understood—"I will lose face."

Though my responsibility to him was merely to practice and to learn, he had one request that he vigorously encouraged me to fulfill—to teach him English. I felt relieved to have something to offer him, so I quickly prepared some beginning materials and rode over to his house for the first lesson. When I got there, he had a tape recorder set up on a small table, along with a pile of oversized paper and a few felt-tip pens from a coloring set. He showed no interest at all in my books, but sat me down next to the recorder and pointed at the pile of paper. On each sheet he had written out in Chinese dozens of phrases, such as "We'll need a spotlight over there," "These mats aren't springy enough," and "Don't worry—it's just a shoulder dislocation." He asked me to write down the English translation next to each phrase, which took a little over two and a half hours. When I was finished, I asked him if he could read my handwriting, and he smiled, saying that he was sure my handwriting was fine. After a series of delicate questions, I determined that he was as yet unfamiliar with the alphabet, so I encouraged him to have a look at my beginning materials. "That's too slow for me," he said. He asked me to repeat each of the phrases I'd written down five times into the recorder, leaving enough time after each repetition for him to say it aloud after me. "The first time should be very slow—one word at a time, with a pause after each word so I can repeat it. The second time should be the same. The third time you should pause after every other word. The fourth time read it through slowly. The fifth time you can read it fast." I looked at the pile of phrase sheets, calculated how much time this would take, and asked if we could do half today and half tomorrow, as dinner was only three hours away. "Don't worry!" he said, beaming. "I've prepared some food for you here. Just tell me when you get hungry." He sat next to me, turned on the machine, then turned it off again. "How do you say, 'And now, Mark will teach me English'?" I told him how and he repeated it, at first slowly, then more quickly, twenty or twenty-one times. He turned the machine on. "And now, Mark will teach me English." I read the first phrase, five times as he had requested, and he pushed a little note across the table. "Better read it six times," it read, "and a little slower."

After several weeks during which we nearly exhausted the phrasal possibilities of our two languages, Pan announced that the time had come to do something new. "Now I want to learn routines." I didn't understand. "Routines?" "Yes. Everything, including language, is like wushu. First you learn the basic moves, or words, then you string them together into routines." He produced from his bedroom a huge sheet of paper made up of smaller pieces taped together. He wanted me to write a story on it. The story he had in mind was a famous Chinese folk tale, "How Yu Gong Moved the Mountain." The story tells of an old man who realized that, if he only had fields where a mountain stood instead, he would have enough arable land to support his family comfortably. So he went out to the mountain with a shovel and a bucket and started to take the mountain down. All his neighbors made fun of him, calling it an impossible task, but Yu Gong disagreed: it would just take a long time, and after several tens of generations had passed, the mountain would at last become a field and his family would live comfortably. Pan had me write this story in big letters, so that he could paste it up on his bedroom wall, listen to the tape I was to make and read along as he lay in bed.

Not only did I repeat this story into the tape recorder several dozen times—at first one word at a time, and so on— but Pan invited Bill, Bob and Marcy over for dinner one night and had them read it a few times for variety. After they had finished, Pan said that he would like to recite a few phrases for them to evaluate and correct. He chose some of his favorite sentences and repeated each seven or eight times without a pause. He belted them out with such fierce concentration we were all afraid to move lest it disturb him. At last he finished and looked at me, asking quietly if it was all right. I nodded and he seemed overcome with relief. He smiled, pointed at me and said to my friends, "I was very nervous just then. I didn't want him to lose face."

While Pan struggled to recite English routines from memory, he began teaching me how to use traditional weapons. He would teach me a single move, then have me practice it in front of him until I could do it ten times in a row without a mistake. He always stood about five feet away from me, with his arms folded, grinding his teeth, and the only time he took his eyes off me was to blink. One night in the late spring I was having a particularly hard time learning a move with the staff. I was sweating heavily and my right hand was bleeding, so the staff had become slippery and hard to control. Several of the athletes stayed on after their workout to watch and to enjoy the breeze that sometimes passed through the training hall. Pan stopped me and indicated that I wasn't working hard enough. "Imagine," he said, "that you are participating in the national competition, and those athletes are your competitors. Look as if you know what you are doing! Frighten them with your strength and confidence." I mustered all the confidence I could, under the circumstances, and flung myself into the move. I lost control of the staff, and it whirled straight into my forehead. As if in a dream, the floor raised up several feet to support my behind, and I sat staring up at Pan while blood ran down across my nose and a fleshy knob grew between my eyebrows. The athletes sprang forward to help me up. They seemed nervous, never having had a foreigner knock himself out in their training hall before, but Pan, after asking if I felt all right, seemed positively inspired. "Sweating and bleeding. Good."

. . .

Every once in a while, Pan felt it necessary to give his students something to think about, to spur them on to greater efforts. During one morning workout two women practiced a combat routine, one armed with a spear, the other with a *dadao*, or halberd. The dadao stands about six feet high and consists of a broadsword attached to a thick wooden pole, with an angry-looking spike at the far end. It is heavy and difficult to wield even for a strong man, so it surprised me to see this young woman, who could not weigh more than one hundred pounds, using it so effectively. At one point in their battle the woman with the dadao swept it toward the other woman's feet, as if to cut them off, but the other woman jumped up in time to avoid the blow. The first woman, without letting the blade of the dadao stop, brought it around in another sweep, as if to cut the other woman in half at the waist. The other woman, without an instant to spare, bent straight from the hips so that the dadao slashed over her back and head, barely an inch away. This combination was to be repeated three times in rapid succession before moving on to the next exchange. The women practiced this move several times, none of which satisfied Pan. "Too slow, and the weapon is too far away from her. It should graze her back as it goes by." They tried again, but still Pan growled angrily. Suddenly he got up and took the dadao from the first woman. The entire training hall went silent and still. Without warming up at all, Pan ordered the woman with the spear to get ready, and to move fast when the time came. His body looked as though electricity had suddenly passed through it, and the huge blade flashed toward her. Once, twice the dadao flew beneath her feet, then swung around in a terrible arc and rode her back with flawless precision. The third time he added a little twist at the end, so that the blade grazed up her neck and sent a little decoration stuck in her pigtails flying across the room.

I had to sit down for a moment to ponder the difficulty of sending an object roughly the shape of an oversized shovel, only heavier, across a girl's back and through her pigtails, without guide ropes or even a safety helmet. Not long before, I had spoken with a former troupe member who, when practicing with this instrument, had suddenly found himself on his knees. The blade, unsharpened, had twirled a bit too close to him and passed through his Achilles' tendon without a sound. Pan handed the dadao back to the woman and walked over to me. "What if you had made a mistake?" I asked. "I never make mistakes," he said, without looking at me.

"Learn calligraphy," Teacher Wei said, "it will improve your mind." So I bought a few brushes, a bottle of ink and some paper, and waited for further instructions.

She gave me a children's book of models to copy from, but beyond a few basic instructions she declined to teach me, saying that her calligraphy was not good enough. "There are plenty of good calligraphers around. Find one and take lessons." I passed word around that I was looking for a calligraphy teacher and not long afterwards heard from Teacher Wu that a suitable teacher had been found. His name was Hai Bin, and he had been born and raised in Suzhou, the city of enclosed gardens, for many centuries famed as an artists' community. Hai Bin had been a prodigy and had studied with many of the city's great painters and calligraphers. I asked Teacher Wu how I should approach him; she told me not to worry, he would visit me in my room that evening.

That afternoon I cleaned my room, set out all my brushes and paper on the desk, and bought some expensive tea to offer him when he arrived. At seven o'clock someone knocked on the door. I opened it, feeling strangely nervous, and sighed with relief when I saw it was only a graduate student about my age, with an English textbook under his arm. I asked if I could help him with anything.

"Are you Mr. Salzman?" he asked, lowering his gaze.

"Yes."

"I am Hai Bin."

At first I didn't believe him, thinking that all good calligraphers had to be old men with thin, white beards. But then I saw a few calligraphy books peeking out from under the English text, so, hiding my disappointment, I invited him in.

While many young men in China were wearing stylish nylon shirts, flared pants and slight heels, and were beginning to let their hair creep down over their ears, Hai Bin wore simple cotton Army pants, a plain white shirt and sandals, and had short hair that looked as if he had cut it himself. He spoke beautiful Mandarin and English, and I noticed that when he sat down at my desk and examined my calligraphy materials, cheap as they were, he handled them with great care. He explained that, no matter what the quality of the brush or paper, one should always treat them as if they were priceless. "This prepares your mind for the serious task ahead." After softening the hairs of a brush in warm water, he dipped it in the ink several times until he felt it was properly loaded. He adjusted himself in the chair, stared quietly at the paper, then brought the brush down on it with the concentration of a surgeon. He spent about five minutes filling the paper with the characters of a poem. When he finished, sweat glistened on his forehead. "Calligraphy is very, very difficult," he said, "because it requires everything." He gave me the brush, took my hand in his, and began showing me how to form the strokes.

In Chinese calligraphy a single dot requires as many as five distinct motions of the wrist and shoulder to be formed properly, and that same dot will be formed differently depending on which of the several tens of established styles you are studying. Once you are able to brush the dots, lines, hooks and circles, you must learn how to put them together into aesthetically balanced characters. After that, you learn to write the separate characters as if an invisible, unbroken line existed between them, to give them continuity and life. There seems to be no end to the complexity of this art; Hai Bin had brought three books, each containing examples of a different calligrapher's work, and we spent an hour comparing their versions of a single character.

He started me copying the work of Liu Gongquan, saying that practicing Liu's vigorous, bold strokes would help my martial arts. Hai Bin believed that calligraphy, painting and wushu were closely related, and that skill in one would inevitably carry over into the others. He told me I should practice every day, but if I could not, I should at least look at the models and run my finger over them as if I were writing them myself. Most important was that I choose a time for practice when I would not be disturbed by friends or sudden noises.

As the weeks passed and I began to make progress, I tired of Liu's models and wanted to try something new. When I told Hai Bin he frowned and said that some people spend their entire lives researching a single model—I should at least be willing to spend a year on this one. At last I convinced him to let me copy one other model, a form of ancient seal script in the style of Wu Changshuo. Hai Bin introduced me to the fundamental brushstrokes of this style, and I found that not one of them resembled those of Liu Gongquan.

Perhaps Hai Bin was right about calligraphy and wushu being related, for although he had had no formal martial arts training he did have a keen eye for what was wrong in my execution of certain moves. On his way to the laboratory in the morning and after dinner in the evening, he would often wander to our little compound where I practiced to point out flaws and to encourage me to work harder. Whenever I stopped to take a break, he would say, "Would Master Pan want you to rest? Your time is precious—use it wisely!" I gave him the nickname Slave Driver, and he seemed very pleased with it. One morning he came earlier than usual, and instead of finding me outside exercising, he looked in my window and saw me practicing calligraphy with a Walkman on. He tapped on the window; I turned around to see him shaking his head and finger at me vigorously, indicating that I should put the Walkman away. After that incident he gave me the nickname Bad Boy.

If there was a painting or calligraphy exhibit in town, Hai Bin would invite me to go with him. We usually began with a bowl of noodles downtown and then made our way to the exhibit, where he would explain the work to me in detail. The only time I saw him truly disgusted was when we saw an exhibit of Chinese calligraphy by a celebrated Frenchman studying in Shanghai, who brushed the characters in a free-form, abstract manner. Hai Bin's face twisted into a grimace. "This is so-called freedom," he said, and wanted to see no more.

During winter break Bill and I traveled to Nanjing and Shanghai, he to visit historical sites and I in search of Western food. In Nanjing I found a restaurant that served chocolate pie and wanted to stay there for the rest of the trip, but Bill convinced me that Shanghai would have better food and besides, we could stop in Suzhou on the way. Hai Bin was home on vacation there and had promised us an insider's tour of the city if we came to visit.

Our train arrived in Suzhou at night. We got on a bus that was empty except for a young couple who were so absorbed in talking to their newborn baby that they did not even notice us. They spoke in Suzhou *hua*, reputedly the most beautiful of Chinese dialects, which sounded distinctly smoother and more nasal than the Changsha hua we were used to. The woman held the baby's face to her throat to keep him warm, while the husband held the baby's two hands in his one. When the bus stopped near our hotel and we stood up, the woman saw us and gasped, holding the baby tighter against her throat and whispering to her husband. He turned to look at us and nearly jumped. Perhaps we looked even stranger than usual, since Bill, at six and a half feet, had to practically bend over at the waist to stand up in the bus, like some sort of crippled giant. We waved to the young family and they smiled nervously, waving goodbye with their baby's hand and telling him to "say goodbye to the foreign uncles."

We walked along a canal with dim lights reflected in its calm surface, following a quiet road lined with trees and two-story wooden houses painted solid black or white and decorated with handsomely carved doors and terraces. By the time we reached our hotel, I had decided that Suzhou was one of the most beautiful cities I had ever seen.

The hotel was not far from where Hai Bin's family lived. At seven o'clock the next morning he met us out front, early morning being the best time to sightsee, since by noon the parks and gardens are jammed with people of all ages, especially children who run, scream and throw fruit peels all over the most serene architecture in the world. Each garden has its own unique theme and characteristics; Hai Bin had spent many hours in the gardens with his teachers, who believed that by simply looking at the careful arrangements of rocks, trees, walls and space, one could improve one's painting and calligraphy. He showed us the best angles from which to view certain famous trees and rocks, some of which have names to describe their particular beauty, and occasionally had us look in a certain direction for several minutes, advising us on how our eyes and minds should move through the scene.

On our third and last day in Suzhou, Hai Bin took us to a small garden that was completely deserted, then asked us to wait for him while he stepped out for a few minutes. He told us that one of his teachers, a distinguished artist now in his eighties, lived nearby and might consent to join us in the garden for the morning. Half an hour later Hai Bin returned with his teacher, who looked more like a sea captain than an artist. He was short, sturdy and unshaven, and had gnarled hands that delivered an extraordinarily powerful handshake. We soon found out why—he carved stone seals, using only a metal knife shaped like a chisel to carve out the designs. His genius, along with the strength and steadiness of his hands, had made him one of the greatest seal artists in China; he had brought along several bound collections of prints made from his seals, which he spread out on a stone table, inviting us to look. In spite of his fame he was thoroughly unpretentious, answering all of our questions with care and enthusiasm, and even offering to carve seals for Bill and me to show his appreciation for our coming to China and teaching English. During our conversation Hai Bin sat quietly next to him, helping him turn the pages and translating for us when we could not understand the artist's dialect.

We asked him about an especially beautiful print depicting two horses leaping together, one in solid color, the other in outline, and he told us that the horses represented him and his late wife. The inscription said something about his thoughts of "journeying to the West," where they would be reunited. Hai Bin explained that in Buddhist terminology the journey West meant the passage of the soul from life into death. Just as he finished his explanation, two *liumang*—punks—wandered noisily into the garden with cigarettes dangling out of their mouths. After looking at Bill and me for a while, talking loudly in dialect so that we could not understand them, they looked down at the collection of seals on the table, dropping ashes on the precious books. They began to jeer at the old man; they read the inscription about the journey to the West and, in their ignorance, accused the old man of sucking up to Westerners. The artist said nothing and sat bent over his books, his eyes lowered, while the hoodlums continued to insult him.

Suddenly Hai Bin stood up. Though slighter than either of the liumang, he turned on them as if they were children and gave them a tongue-lashing that apparently ended with the advice that they leave the garden, for that is what they did, grinning nervously. Hai Bin gently brushed the ashes off his teacher's book and apologized to Bill and me for their behavior. The artist apologized also, telling us how ashamed he felt to see young people acting so rudely, then asked us to excuse him, for it was getting late and he had to return home. We took a few photographs together, said farewell and watched as they left the garden, Hai Bin carrying the master's books and supporting his arm as they walked.

Later that day in another garden, Hai Bin and I stood on a little bridge arching over an artificial pond. We were looking at a pair of Mandarin ducks swimming under a plaque that extolled the virtues of their species, which chooses only one mate and remains devoted to it for life. I asked Hai Bin if this was true and he answered, "Yes, of course. But I've heard that if you take them to America, they ask for a divorce within a few months." This was the first joke I had heard in China, so I felt it was some kind of breakthrough. I responded by telling him a few American jokes, and he laughed, but pointed out that most of them were biologically unfeasable.

Back in Changsha I was determined to pursue our friendship. Although we liked each other very much and had become familiar, our conversations still sounded like interviews for a Cultural Exchange magazine. We shared many interests, and I had seen his home and met his family, who were much like my own. Surely, I thought, at heart we could not be so different. One warm night I bought two bottles of beer and asked Hai Bin to come down to the river to watch the sunset with me. We talked about calligraphy and medicine until it got dark; then I pulled out the beers and we polished them off, sitting on the floodwall and watching the cigarettes of the fishermen glowing like red fireflies. We were laughing about something when suddenly it flashed through my mind what was missing from our discussions.

"Hai Bin, tell me—what are the two things you think about most, that pass through your mind most, whether you like it or not?"

He paused for a few seconds, scratching his head, then answered "Eating and sleeping."

I was so full of hope that our culture gap would magically be bridged that I could not accept this.

"Come on, Hai Bin, that can't be true!"

"But of course it is true! The food in our dining hall is so terrible it makes me think of home, when my mother cooked for me. I think of it all the time. Don't you always tell me how much you dream of milk trembles?"

"Milk shakes."

"Milk shakes. And our dormitory is very noisy at night, because the students laugh loudly and listen to the Voice of America with the radios on loudly, and I cannot go to sleep when I want, so I never get enough sleep."

I realized, to my disappointment, that he was being sincere, and when he put the question to me I became flustered.

"Well, Hai Bin, I guess I want people to like me, for one thing. Especially women—do you know what I mean?"

"And the other?"

"I want to be very, very good at something."

"At what?"

"It doesn't matter, I guess. I want to do something well

enough that I feel satisfied with it, or get some kind of recognition for it."

He looked at me curiously. "Why do you think about these things?"

"Because they are important—aren't they?"

"Yes," he said, "but these goals can be achieved so easily! All you have to do is be kind and work hard. But to eat and sleep well, that is a difficult wish, because you cannot control these things yourself."

In one of my classes I read aloud "The Lottery" by Shirley Jackson, a short story about a small town that holds an annual lottery. Participation is compulsory for residents of the town, and the "winner" is stoned to death. No one knows why the lottery is held or how the tradition began, but no one questions it. Even the victim, when her number is finally called, seems blind to the madness of it all: as the crowd falls upon her, she cries that the choice was not fair, she should have had another chance. When I finished reading the story, a particularly opinionated student raised her hand.

"Teacher Mark," she asked, with a mixture of confusion and disgust in her voice, "why did people in America do that?"

I explained, perhaps too quickly, that this was a fictional story, but she did not seem convinced.

"It must be based on some kind of experience, or else how could she think of it?" she asked, giving me a knowing look. I said that the story gave us an exaggerated and therefore dramatic example of a kind of behavior that occurs all over the world, not just in America, where individuals do terrible things, things they would ordinarily never do, when they are part of a crowd.

"But who," she replied, "would be so foolish, to have a lottery and kill someone? No one in China can believe such a story! You Americans have big imaginations!"

And you Chinese have short memories, I was thinking, when a man sitting behind her proved me wrong.

"I have seen something like this," he said. "During the

Cultural Revolution. Everyone wanted to show love for Chairman Mao—everyone had to—so we went to the river. Chairman Mao swam across the Yangtse River, did you know that? So we all thought we should swim across the Xiang River. Many people jumped in—thousands of people—but a terrible, terrible thing happened. Too many people jumped in at once, they pushed to get in the water, so there was not enough room to swim. You could not move your arms! The river looked like soup, and all the peoples' heads looked like dumplings going up and down. Because they could not move their arms, many people sank to the bottom and died. Really —they looked like dumplings."

The woman frowned. "That is not the same at all! That was an accident. Those people did not intend to hurt each other when they jumped in! In this story, the village people know they are killing the woman. They are throwing stones at her!"

An awkward silence followed her comment. She fidgeted in her seat, then at last sighed with exasperation.

"Anyway, we have all seen terrible things," she said. "Why must we read about them? Can't you give us stories that have happy endings?"

"There is a lab technician in our college," Hai Bin said one afternoon, "who wants to meet you. He practices wushu and says that his teacher is interested in you. If you like, his teacher will give you lessons to supplement Master Pan's instruction." Hai Bin told me I could meet the technician, Little Guo, in his lab that evening. "I will tell you something, though," Hai Bin said. "Little Guo is a nice man, but he is sometimes clumsy—he often breaks things by accident. Perhaps he cannot control his strength. So if you practice with him, be careful he does not hurt you by mistake."

That night I made my way up to the second floor of the research building, stumbling over a spittoon placed in the dark stairway. When I knocked on the door, a voice said, "Just a minute—" then a young man who stood a full head taller than me, with huge shoulders and long arms that seemed to reach to his knees, opened the door. "I'm Little Guo," he said, shaking my teeth loose with a handshake that engaged his entire upper body. He invited me into his lab, which was crowded with thirty or more low stools. As I walked in, I sensed movement all around me, but it took a few seconds for me to sort out what I was seeing. On each stool crouched three mice, nervously sniffing at the edges of the stools, occasionally peering over as if getting ready to jump.

"Mice!" Little Guo said, slapping me hard on the shoulder and beaming. He explained that his current experiment involved tagging and weighing a large number of mice in groups of three to test their resistance to a certain disease. "But won't they jump off?" I asked him. "No—they are afraid of heights! I've tried it before."

As he weighed the mice, he told me that his teacher, Zheng, was an expert *nei-gong* boxer. Nei-gong, literally meaning "internal skill," refers to the schools of martial arts such as Taijiquan that emphasize the cultivation of *qi*, "intrinsic energy," or "internal force," rather than physical strength. I had by that time seen countless demonstrations of qi, none of which impressed me as being anything more than demonstrations of sleight of hand, confidence, or good balance, so I told Little Guo that I was skeptical. "Oh, but it is real!" he said, "You will see it yourself! Let me take you to Master Zheng's house, and he will show you." We set a date for the next week, and were just agreeing on a place to meet, when suddenly it happened. One of the mice had overcome its fear of heights and jumped to the floor, where it ran about at full speed, squeaking with abandon. The other mice immediately became excited, leaning farther out over the edges of the stools than before and following the movements of the free mouse with their eyes and ears.

"Aiya!" Little Guo cried, charging at the mouse but missing it. The mouse darted and skidded under the stools as Little Guo followed it, finally stopping in a corner of the room under a lab table. Little Guo crept slowly toward it, his giant, rough hands cupped to grab the mouse. I didn't want to look, for I had a feeling that Little Guo would land on the mouse and crush it, but before he sprang, the mouse shot out to the left and escaped. Little Guo spun around to follow it and hit one of the stools with his forearm, propelling three more mice into freedom. The mice still on the stools became frenzied, and one by one began jumping to the floor.

·   ·   ·

One week later Little Guo took me to Master Zheng's house. Zheng lived in a factory unit that had its own electrical generator, so although most of the city was blacked out that night, his unit had electricity. Zheng, his wife, his three-year-old daughter and three of his senior students were finishing dinner when I arrived. At first Zheng was very stiff. Perhaps he was anxious not to lose the respect of his students by appearing too excited over a visit from a foreigner. After we drank a few glasses of a precious medicinal wine, though, he became not only friendly but very entertaining. He had a remarkable talent for mimicry, which he attributed to his many years of training with the Changsha "Flower Drum Opera" company. Flower Drum Opera, peculiar to Hunan, is sung in Hunan dialect and uses costumes and themes quite different from the more well-known Peking Opera. Both his parents had been Flower Drum singers, as had his wife, and all of his brothers and sisters were still performing. I never learned why Zheng himself had left the opera, getting a job in a factory and concentrating on martial arts in his spare time.

Unlike many of my acquaintances at the medical college, Zheng and his students were all natives of Changsha and wanted to know what I thought of Changsha habits, food and language. I was accustomed to hearing, from people born in other parts of China, that in Changsha "there is nothing to do, nothing to buy, the people have no manners, the food is terrible and their dialect sounds awful." Zheng, however, insisted that although Changsha was a poor city, its natives were the most polite, its food the most peppery and its dialect the most lively in all of China, so I should feel lucky indeed to have been sent there. We drank to that, and then it was time for martial arts.

We went up to the roof of the building, which had a breathtaking view of the river and the main part of the city to the south. The blackout made the city look deserted except for small bonfires and candles flickering in the streets, where families played *mahjong* and poker. Zheng asked me to show him and his students the routines that Pan had taught me. I went through three of them and was rewarded with applause and shouts of "Manhaodilei!" the Changshahua phrase meaning "very good." Zheng said that my Shaolin boxing looked very strong, and no wonder, he said, with a teacher like Pan Qingfu.

"But have you ever studied Wudang boxing?" he asked.

"Wudang boxing?"

"Shaolin boxing belongs to what we call the hard schools, or external schools. They are fast and strong. Wudang boxing belongs to what we call the soft schools, or nei-gong. Wudang Mountain is the site of a famous Taoist temple, where Taijiquan, Baguazhang and Xingyiquan, the three internal schools, are practiced. Have you ever studied them?"

"I'm afraid not."

"Well, you should. Watch!"

He went through a routine of Chen style Taijiquan, writhing and twisting over the roof in slow motion, occasionally lashing out with a punch or kick that shook his entire body. The motion of his hips and abdomen looked fluid and dance-like. I had never seen anything like it. Then he challenged me to try to hold on to him. I reached out and grabbed his arms, but with a twist of his hips and shoulders he was free. Again and again I tried to hold him still, but no matter how much strength I used he managed to wriggle free without much difficulty. He challenged me to hit him in the chest, so I lunged forward with a straight right and his chest seemed to collapse, disappearing just as I thought I would hit him in the ribs. He stood with his back to a wall and told me to hold him against the wall, which I did, but with a shake and a twist he escaped. After a few more of these demonstrations we went back downstairs to rest and have some more food and wine. When we had settled down to eat and drink, he asked me why I thought he could do all those things.

"You are very skilled," I answered, but he did not appear flattered.

"It's not skill! It is qi," he said, giving me a mysterious look.

I asked him if he could explain qi for me, as I had heard about it for many years but had never had a clear idea of what it was.

"Qi is a kind of force that resides in the lower abdomen and circulates through the body. A soft-boxing master can direct it to any part of his body, or even out of his body to another person's body. That is why you could not hold me. In the old days, masters were so good they could hurt or heal you without even touching you. Do you believe this?"

I told him that although I certainly believed that I could not hold onto him, I had to admit that I did not believe that a mysterious force circulates through the body.

"Oh, no?" he said, his eyes widening with excitement. "Then explain this!"

Sitting on a low ceramic stool he picked up a small wooden chair and held it above his head. His wife started to say something, but Zheng hushed her and, looking straight at me, brought the chair down with all his might onto his head. The chair broke.

He held the smashed chair out for me to examine, then asked me to explain it. "Whatever it is, Master Zheng, it is certainly impressive."

"I should have married a carpenter," his wife grumbled.

Zheng said that I was perfectly right to be skeptical about qi—that way I would not easily be fooled by charlatans. The only way to experience qi, he said, was to cultivate it yourself, so he kindly offered to teach me on the condition that I try to be open-minded and to obey his instructions to the word. Starting that night, and three nights a week thereafter, Zheng taught me the rudiments of nei-gong.

My lessons with Zheng differed in many ways from my lessons with Pan. The moment I entered Pan's training hall I could feel his eyes telling me, "There is so little time—don't waste an instant!" He paced around me as I warmed up, and as soon as I said "Ready," he locked his eyes on mine and said, "Begin!" He believed that effort, concentration, stamina and desire were the ingredients of a proper training. When I asked him the difference between a great fighter and a mediocre one, he said, "Mediocre fighters are lazy and try to cover up for it with superstition. Masters eat bitter every day of their lives, and that's that." In all of our lessons he mentioned qi only once, and even then he used it in its original meaning, breath: "Don't hold your breath when you practice," he said, "or you'll get tired." Pan had great respect for the internal styles of wushu—he taught and practiced them all—but he respected them for their technical and theoretical sophistication, saying that no martial art could give one supernatural powers. "If the masters in the old days could really jump thirty feet high," he snarled, "then why the hell did they build staircases in their houses?"

Zheng had a different approach. Lessons began with a glass of herbal wine and conversation; he had a warm, fatherly relationship with his students, and one could see that they were all very fond of him. If it was not raining or too misty out, we went up to the roof to practice. Zheng said that rain and mist seeped in through the pores of the skin and damaged one's qi, so it was best not to practice on days like that. On the roof, training was very casual. Each student worked on his own while Zheng walked back and forth among them, every once in a while calling everyone together to watch a certain technique. His students practiced in short bursts, taking frequent rests to avoid breaking a sweat. All of them, including Zheng, thought I was self-destructive, drilling to the point of exhaustion every night, and said that I would learn in the long run that the Taoist attitude of moderation was the most effective. In addition to forms, breathing exercises and sparring, Zheng's training included a method of conditioning the hands. From a wooden frame on the roof he hung three coarse burlap bags filled with sand, each weighing at least a hundred pounds, and had us punch them for twenty minutes or so every day. This method differed from Pan's iron fist training in several ways: Zheng's method rubbed the knuckles raw, developing thick callous tissue over them in only six to eight months. The callus made Zheng's hands look swollen, so one could barely distinguish one knuckle from the other. Pan's method of hitting the iron plate had to be done more carefully, as the danger to the hand was greater, and the results appeared much more slowly. It took several years to develop the proper calluses, which looked as if they had been riveted onto the knuckles. Hoping to please both teachers I practiced both methods, giving me scabs on the surface of my hands from the sandbags and blood clots under the skin from hitting the iron.

After a few months had passed, Zheng invited me to join him on a day trip to a small city south of Changsha. He had a good friend there, he said, whom he wanted me to meet.

"My friend is a sculptor, an artist. In his spare time he makes swords. He is my best friend, and as he is feeling lonely these days, he wants me to visit. I think if you come, it will cheer him up. If he likes you, he might even make a sword for you." That Sunday Zheng, three of his students and I got on a crowded bus that followed a dusty road through the countryside for three hours, stopping finally in a city that looked even more depressing than Changsha. On our way to catch a local bus, Zheng stopped at a peddlar's cart and bought something wrapped in pieces of newspaper. He unfolded the newspapers and distributed some dark, shiny objects that looked like walnut shells among his students, then offered me one.

"Binglang," he said, popping one into his mouth. "It's a local specialty."

Not wanting to be rude I put the binglang into my mouth. It seemed to be a kind of nutshell steeped in a strong cinnamon extract that slowly became pliable and fibrous as I chewed. I like cinnamon very much, so I chewed the object until it had no more flavor, then swallowed it with difficulty.

"Do you want another one?" Zheng asked.

"Yes, thank you. It is very good."

Zheng and the other students looked pleased that I enjoyed this little treat, so at the next binglang cart they argued over who would have the honor of treating me to more of them. Altogether I ate seven or eight of them, thinking this might be our only lunch. On the bus, Zheng asked me if I wanted any more binglang, and I answered that I was full enough for the time being. His eyes opened wide and he asked me if I had swallowed them.

"Yes—wasn't I supposed to?"

"Aiya . . ." he gasped, then told the others what I had done. They all looked at me in amazement and I suddenly became very nervous. My heart started beating wildly, and I asked if I had eaten something poisonous. They all laughed at this;

Zheng said that the binglang was not poisonous, but was meant to be chewed, not swallowed. "Binglang is like wine," he said, "it makes you feel a little drunk. We thought you were used to it, and that was why you chewed so many. Just one or two of them makes us feel dizzy!" The jolt of adrenaline I had just experienced must have quickened the effect of the drug, which is known as betel nut in the West, for my legs began to feel long and rubbery, a buzzing filled my ears, and the bus ride, which lasted only fifteen minutes or so, seemed to go on for over an hour.

We got off in the middle of a community of cement apartment buildings laid out in rows that went on in all directions as far as the eye could see. We walked north for eight or nine blocks and at last approached one of the dark entryways. Zheng called out a name, someone shouted back in response, and a minute later a short man with a bouncing, agitated gait ran out to meet us. After shaking hands and exchanging loud, emotional greetings with Zheng, Lin stood in front of me and looked me over. "So you are the man my friend has told me about—welcome to my home!" He shook my hand vigorously, almost violently, taking my arm into his other hand and grasping it tightly, winking at me as if something of great significance were taking place that need not be put into words; he seemed to be on the verge of tears. I was still disoriented from the betel nut and was unable to tell if the man's behavior was really strange or if I was imagining things. This filled me with confusion, and once again my heart raced and adrenaline rushed through me. I felt slightly nauseous and asked to sit down, afraid that I might pass out or throw up at any moment. Once we got inside the apartment, Zheng and his friend disappeared into the kitchen, leaving Zheng's three students and me in the dining room to relax and have tea. I asked them if Lin seemed a little excited to them. They smiled and assured me that he was always "a little crazy," but that I should not worry—he had a good heart, and a more loyal friend could not be found. This came as a great relief to me, and almost immediately I felt my head beginning to clear.

A few other friends from the neighborhood trickled in, moving back and forth between the kitchen and the dining room as they helped to cook and to set the table. At about one o'clock the feast began, with fifteen of us sitting at a big, round table carried over from a nearby factory. Lin sat next to me and kept my bowl full the whole time, encouraging me to eat with hearty slaps on the back. Every five minutes or so he lifted up his wine glass to toast someone, so that after an hour had passed, everyone was very red in the face. The more Lin drank the more excited he became, talking in dialect too quickly for me to understand, but with emotions that were easy to read. He alternated between slamming the table and cursing with rage, murmuring softly in a trembling voice, as if terribly depressed, then turning to me and declaring with a shout that friendship was everything, it was all that mattered. This cycle of emotions became more exaggerated as time went on and more wine was consumed. Everyone else at the table seemed to be there to listen to him, agree with him, console him or support him as his mood required. At one point when he looked depressed, Zheng suggested that he show me some of his artwork. Lin jumped up and ran into an adjacent room, from which he emerged with a tiny clay sculpture of a naked man, hunched over in despair. It was a haunting sculpture, and I asked if he had any others to show me.

"No," he sighed, "I've given away everything else. I give away all of my work. But there is one thing I have that I will never give away—it is my treasure, my most precious thing.

Do you want to see it?" I said that I would like to, and he produced from a desk drawer a single postcard with a photograph of Michelangelo's David on its face. It was yellowed and badly worn from many years of handling.

"Michelangelo is my teacher," he said, "and this is my lesson book. It is all I have to work from. This sculpture, the David, is perfect, and I dream of it all the time. If I could see this sculpture with my own eyes and touch it with my fingers, I think I would die from happiness!" He carefully returned the postcard to the drawer, then burst into another angry monologue that I could not understand. By this time he was very drunk. He stood up, picked up an elaborate letter opener, pointed to it emphatically and rushed toward the door. He pretended to have trouble opening it, giving his friends time to catch him and take the letter opener away from him. He made a show of protest, struggling weakly to break free, but it was clearly for form's sake, and no one except me seemed particularly alarmed. While Lin's friends calmed him down, Zheng took me outside for a walk.

"I'm sorry about this," he said. "I'm very sorry that your day has been unpleasant." I said that there was no need to apologize, but perhaps he could explain what was going on, since I was beginning to fear that I was the cause of the trouble.

"No, no—not at all! Lin likes you very much! I think you have cheered him up by coming. I'll tell you what is wrong. Lin is a very emotional man, an unusual man. He is very talented and smart, and he is my best friend. If you are his friend, I tell you that he would die for you, his loyalty is so great. During a period of hard times, he once saved my life. But sometimes he cannot control his emotions. He was married for a long time to a mean woman. After years and years of trouble, they were finally granted a divorce. Divorce, you know, is extremely rare in China. But Lin, even though he hates her, still loves her, too. That sounds impossible, but it is true. Anyway, she is getting remarried to someone else, and Lin is very upset. He promised he would not interfere, but not long ago he heard that the woman is having the wedding party only four blocks down the road—that building right there! Well, today is the wedding—they are over there right now. So we have come to cheer Lin up and make sure he doesn't do anything stupid. Lin doesn't want to make trouble —he asked us to come—but you see, being the way he is, I guess he can't help getting worked up about it. I assure you, though, he is not a bad or a violent man. He is gentle, but today he is very upset. I'm sorry if this has frightened you."

When we went back inside, Lin once again sat at the head of the table, looking much better, and gestured for me to sit next to him. "I'm sorry for making so much noise," he said. "The important thing is, I have all my good friends with me, and now I have a new friend, an American friend. Tell me about sculpture in America—what does it look like?" I was tempted to say "ridiculous," but instead I confessed that I did not know enough about the subject to give him a proper answer. "If you like, though, I could ask my family to send an illustrated book about it." Lin nodded appreciatively, then froze as if he had just seen an apparition. "Do you mean," he asked in a whisper, "that it would be possible . . . to send a book of photographs here from your country? It would pass through customs?"

"Certainly, if it were addressed to me. Then I could have Master Zheng take it to you, in case I don't see you again."

He held my arm tight and looked closely at me, his eyes wild with hope.

"Are there books like that . . . about Michelangelo?"

"Yes, there are, and I will get one for you."

I thought he would surely cry with joy, but instead he drew himself up straight, nodded as if casually interested, and busied himself pouring wine for his friends.

"Good—good. Yes, that would be very good if you could do that, but if it is too much trouble, of course . . ."

"No, it would not be too much trouble at all."

"I don't want to trouble you. You needn't be polite."

"Not at all. It will be easy to arrange."

"Ah, well. . . . But if you can't get the book, don't worry about it. Sometimes, you know, a thing can seem easy one day and impossible the next."

Two months later I had a beautiful, soft-cover *Michelangelo* in my hands, but there was a problem. Not long after my visit to the sculptor's home, I heard a rumor that Zheng's students resented the special attention Zheng gave me, and felt that the content of their lessons had been rearranged to focus on my needs. There was no way of knowing if the rumor was true, but to be safe I asked Zheng if I might continue at a less feverish pace, and cut my lessons down to once or twice a week. He reacted strangely; he asked if I fully appreciated the risks he was taking by accepting me as a student, and said that if I was dissatisfied with the effort he was making to teach me I should just say so. I decided not to press the matter and continued seeing him three times a week, but after that he paid increasingly close attention to me during the lessons, and almost completely ignored his other students.

One night none of the other students showed up. I asked after them and Zheng said that he had told them not to come so often, that they would be around forever but I would not, and he wanted to make sure I felt satisfied with his instruction. When I heard this I felt sick with regret, and told him right away that under those circumstances I could not pos-

sibly feel comfortable being his student. An expression somewhere between anger and fear passed over his face, and he
blurted out that obviously I did not understand how
important this arrangement was to him, and that I should not
think only of myself.

When he said this I felt bad, and I apologized for seeming
ungrateful. Afterwards, though, this incident went through
my mind again and again, and the more I tried to sort it
out, the more confusing it became. At last I spoke to Hai Bin
about it. He listened carefully, then told me that I should
not feel angry or guilty, that it was no one's fault, but that in
this case, my being a foreigner was simply "too inconvenient."
He helped me draft a polite letter thanking Zheng for his
generosity and kindness, then stating that unfortunately, due
to an increase in my responsibilities at the college, I could no
longer continue my lessons.

I found Little Guo and showed him the *Michelangelo*
book, asking if he could take it to Zheng to pass on to his
friend Lin.

Little Guo shook his head. "Under these conditions, it
would be impossible. Lin, as a matter of face, would not accept it, because you have insulted Zheng by discontinuing
your lessons. You will have to give it to someone else. How
sad!"

"Isn't there some way we could get the book to him without involving Zheng?" I asked, unable to believe that the
book, having traveled twelve thousand miles, could not find
its way a hundred miles more.

"Mei banfa"—there is no way—he answered. "Just as Lin
said, easy things become impossible. Most things are like
that." Suddenly Little Guo smiled, then laughed out loud.
"And impossible things become easy! I never imagined that

the mice in my lab would jump! Do you remember how we chased them for almost two hours?"

I was too upset to laugh with him. He sensed my mood and patted me on the shoulder. "Don't worry about it. Do you know the story of the old man and the horse? It's a famous Chinese story, we all learn it when we are children. An old man's horse runs away one day. His friends all say they are sorry to hear about the horse, but the old man says, 'I'm not worried about it. You never know what happens.' Sure enough, a few days later the horse returns, leading a whole herd of wild horses back with it. Everyone congratulates the old man on his good fortune, but the old man just says, 'You never know what happens,' and doesn't make a big deal out of it. And sure enough, his only son becomes crippled in an accident while training one of the horses. Everyone says how sorry they are to hear the sad news, but the old man says, 'You never know what happens.' And not long afterward government troops pass through the village looking for healthy young men to recruit for a border campaign. Of course, the old man's son is passed over because of his injuries. This is the Chinese way of thinking. Speaking honestly, it seems to me that you foreigners get terribly sentimental about little things."

1 had walked along the river many times since meeting the fisherman that day in winter, but I did not see him again until spring. It was late afternoon, and I had bicycled to a point along the river about a mile downstream from where we had met, hoping to find a deserted spot to draw a picture. I found a niche in the sloping floodwall and started drawing a junk moored not far from me. Half an hour passed, and just as I finished the drawing, I heard someone calling my Chinese name. I looked down to see Old Ding scrambling up the flood-wall, his boat anchored behind him. I noticed that he limped badly, and when he got up close I could see that one of his legs was shorter than the other and set at an odd angle. Such was his balance and skill in the boats that I only saw his deformity when he came ashore. He squatted down beside me and explained that he had just returned from a long fishing trip on Dong Ting, a sprawling lake in North Hunan. "Big fish up there," he said, gesturing with his arms. Then he asked me what I was doing. I showed him the drawing, and his face lit up. "Just like it! Just like the boat!" He cupped his hands to his mouth and yelled something in the direction of the junk, and right away a family appeared on deck. "Let's show it to them!" he said, and dragged me down to the water. He exchanged a few words with the family, and they leapt into action, the women going into the sheltered part of the junk to prepare food and the men rowing out to meet us in one of two tiny boats lashed to the side. We got in the little boat and returned with them to the junk. We ate a few snacks of differ-ent kinds of salted fish, had tea, and then I showed them the

drawing. They seemed delighted by it, so I tore the sheet out of my block. I handed it to the oldest member of the family, a man in his sixties, who opened his eyes wide with surprise and would not take it, saying, "How can I take this? It is a work of art; what do I have to offer you in return?" I laughed, saying that it was only a drawing, and I would be happy if he would take it just for fun. But he was serious; when at last he accepted it, putting it down carefully on the bed, he began negotiating with Old Ding to choose an appropriate gift for me.

Fifteen minutes of vigorous discussion, all in dialect, produced a decision: they would give me one of the rowboats. I looked at Old Ding and said that that was absolutely ridiculous, that of course I would not take a boat from a poor fisherman's family in return for a charcoal sketch. "Oh, but it's no problem! They can get a new one!" I realized that the situation was serious, for if I refused and left, they would no doubt carry the rowboat to my house and lay it on the front porch. I looked at the old man. "That is a very fine gift, it is worth thousands of drawings like that one, but we Americans have a custom, and that is we speak directly. If we want something, we say so." Many Chinese people appreciate "talking straight," perhaps because convention almost never allows it, so they applauded this and told me by all means to speak up. "The boat is very fine, but there is something I want more." They all smiled and nodded and said that of course I could have whatever I wanted, but I could see they were deeply nervous. I believe they expected me to ask for the junk. "In my country, we have a superstition. If someone gives you a piece of art, like a painting or a poem, you must give him a piece of art in return, or the feeling will be spoiled. If I take the boat, I will feel sad. I would prefer that a member of your family sing a folk song from your hometown." The family, almost hysterical with relief, cheered my decision, saying it had "true spirit," and each of them sang something for me.

After we left the junk, Old Ding asked me if I would have dinner with his family that night. I wasn't feeling up to it just then; the encounter with the family on the junk had tired me out, so we made a date for a week from that day, a Saturday. I was to wait by the river in the afternoon, and he would pick me up in his boat.

I brought my cello and an album of photographs of my family. I attracted a certain amount of attention as I stood next to the water with the hard case strapped to my back. By the time Old Ding came, a crowd had gathered. They watched me climb on, and the two of us pushed off and rowed downstream. The crowd followed us on the bank until I smiled and waved. They all smiled and waved back, nodded as if something had been explained, then turned and disappeared over the floodwall. As we rowed, the sun went down. Soon only the silhouettes of factory smokestacks and low hills could be seen through the copper-grey haze. We stopped near a cluster of other boats, all moored against the wall near a stairway leading up to the street. We left the river and walked for about fifteen minutes through a maze of narrow, dark alleys, arriving finally at a row of three-story concrete buildings. We entered a pitch-black doorway and felt our way up the stairs. Then he stopped me, and I heard him knock on a wooden door. The door opened into a small room illuminated by three candles. "No electricity tonight," Old Ding said. It took a few seconds for me to orient myself to this eerie scene, but I soon began to recognize members of his family I'd met that morning in winter. I heard only gentle murmurs from the children who were seeing me for the first time. They asked me to stand next to a candle so they could see me clearly.

After that they passed a candle around, holding it in front of each of their faces so I could see them properly, too, and Old Ding introduced them to me in turn. There were his four cousins, three aunts, three uncles, two nieces, his wife and two children, his two brothers and one sister-in-law, his father and his grandmother. In the doorway stood a few friends of the family who had been waiting across the hall when I came in. Everyone sat on the floor except for his father and his grandmother, who sat on the two chairs in the room. The father got up and, taking me by the arm, insisted that I take his seat next to his mother. He went into the kitchen and came back with a bottle of baijiu and a bowl of peanuts.

The most striking figures in the room were the grandmother and the brother, the one who had helped row me back that day. The grandmother had brilliant white hair, carefully combed and tied back, and sparkling eyes that looked at me without blinking. She wore thick cotton trousers and a padded cotton jacket, all black, and though worn threadbare, her clothes were spotless. She sat only a few inches away from me, absorbed in pure wonder. She had great dignity nonetheless, occasionally turning her head as if to show me her profile in the candlelight. Fu Manchu sat on the floor right in front of her, like some sort of gargoyle, grinning demonically and waiting for someone to try and attack her. I tried talking to these two, but they didn't understand my Mandarin, and I didn't understand their dialect, so we just looked at each other while I ate the peanuts and drank with the father.

I took the album out of my bag and showed them their first color photographs. The clarity and brilliance of the prints overwhelmed them; several minutes passed before anyone asked about the people in them. Two pictures impressed them above all. One showed four generations of my family seated in my grandmother's living room in front of an elaborate drapery—the drapery looked unimaginably beautiful, they said. The other picture showed my other grandmother standing with my mother. "This is your grandmother?" they asked. "How old is she?" They all clicked their tongues with disbelief when I told them, and when I pointed out my mother, they shook their heads. "She is too young to be your mother, she is a young girl. And this one you call your grandmother, she looks thirty years old." I asked them what made these women look so young to them. "It's easy—they are wearing such beautiful clothes. Only young women wear bright colors. And they are smiling! Old ladies never smile in pictures."

At length the grandmother said something to me and pointed to the cello case. I noticed that all the children had moved as far away from it as possible, so that it sat in an empty circle in the middle of the floor. "She wants to know what it is," Old Ding said. I told him it was a *datiqin*, a cello. He passed this on to everyone, they discussed something, then he turned back to me. "What's a cello?" I went over to the case and opened it, whereupon the children shrieked with terror, and two of them started to cry. Old Ding, between fits of laughter, explained, "My brother told them you had a spirit inside it that eats children!" I looked at Fu Manchu, and he nodded enthusiastically. I took the cello out of the case and the whole room gasped, clicked their tongues and sighed with appreciation. I walked over to my seat and began to explain the mechanics of the instrument, and then I noticed that none of them were looking at me or the cello. "It's beautiful," they kept saying, and one by one they all went to touch the divine object—the red velvet lining inside the cello case.

After the touching of the velvet, they asked to hear the instrument. I tuned it up, waited until they were ready, and began to play Bach's First Suite for Unaccompanied Cello. The instant I drew the bow over the strings, the family started

talking with one another, in full voice, mostly about the velvet. I thought perhaps I had misunderstood and they didn't
want me to play, so I stopped. Gradually they became silent
and looked at me. "Why did you stop?" I felt puzzled, but
started again. Right away they resumed their conversations,
the children laughed and played with the case, and Fu Manchu
initiated an arm wrestle with the third brother. When I finished the first movement, they looked at me again. "Is that
all?" I must admit that I felt disappointed that their first
exposure to the cello, and to Bach, was generating so little
interest. But then I remembered what a Chinese friend had
told me one night at a performance of instrumental music
where the audience talked, laughed, spat and walked around
during the show. I mentioned to him that the audience
seemed unbelievably rude, and he answered that, on the con-
trary, this showed they were enjoying it. He said that for the
majority of Chinese who are peasants and laborers, music is
enjoyed as a sort of background entertainment and is intended
as an accompaniment to *renao*, which means literally "heat
and noise." Renao is the Chinese word for good fun, the kind
you might have at an amusement park in America, and noise
and movement are essential to it.

I accompanied their renao for as long as I could stand it,
then put the cello away. The grandmother spoke again, and
this time I understood her. "Sing a song." My mind went
blank; after several minutes of stalling, the only song I could
think of was the first stanza of "Scarborough Fair." Singing
affected them differently, for they listened in complete silence.
When I finished, the grandmother tapped me on the shoulder
with her tiny finger. "Sing it again." I sang it again, and she
asked me to sing it one more time. "She likes the song," Old
Ding told me, and he encouraged me to keep singing it until
dinner was ready. The children spared me from that task by

squealing with disapproval, saying that we had all heard enough music, now it was time for a ghost story. "Could you do that for them?" Old Ding asked. "They think you could tell a good one, because you look like a ghost yourself." I said I would be happy to, but only if the children sat close enough for me to touch them, knowing that this would add to the dramatic effect. It took a while for them to get up the courage, but in time I had a circle of trembling children around my feet, waiting to be terrified. The children had heard enough Mandarin on the loudspeakers and in school, so that if I spoke slowly, they understood. I created a horrible tale about a hungry ghost that hid in dark corners of houses or under beds, waiting to nibble at the ankles of little boys and girls, that had golden hair, strange blue eyes and a long, narrow nose. Upon hearing this description, they began edging away from me. "Would you like me to show you how the ghost nibbles?" I asked, and the entire circle of them vaporized, and could only be seen peeking out at me from behind doors for the rest of the evening.

This amused everyone, but most of all Fu Manchu, who growled with delight and tried to capture the children and carry them back toward me. They scratched, kicked and bit him, which only added to his enjoyment. This could have gone on all night if my friend's wife hadn't stuck her head in to announce dinner. We all herded into a storage room on the first floor, which they had cleared out for dinner, and sat at three low tables, using overturned washbasins as chairs.

They served five or six varieties of dried fish, a stew of fresh fish and Chinese parsley, and some sausage, along with rice scooped out of a huge black iron pot. There was a large bowl of fresh hot peppers mixed with crushed dried peppers on each table. A pinch on my rice was enough for me, but only whole mouthfuls satisfied my hosts, who considered the peppers a separate dish rather than a seasoning. Tea followed, and I noticed that most of them ate the leaves after drinking the tea. Suddenly Fu Manchu leapt to his feet and said something in an excited voice. Everyone got up and cleared the tables, moved them and all the washbasins out of the storage room, then returned to squat against the walls. The brother grinned at me, flashing his teeth and saying something I could not understand. Old Ding tapped me on the shoulder. "He wants to show you how strong he is. Watch!" The brother stripped to the waist, revealing a massive chest and arms muscled with steel bands. He jumped face-first to the ground and started doing push-ups on his fingertips while the rest of the family counted aloud. At seventy-five, with no signs of slowing down, he jumped back up, assumed a martial stance and punched the air in front of him one hundred times. He looked as though he were in some sort of frenzy, and after the punches he took a cloth soaked in cold water and squeezed it over his head, dancing with joy as the icy drops ran down his back. "Now it is your turn. Show him how strong you are, then you two can wrestle!" I chose to keep my shirt on, the temperature being forty degrees or so in their unheated building, and not to begin my demonstration with push-ups. I performed a routine of Chinese Southern Fist, which can be done in a very small area, embellishing it with one or two jumping kicks that I knew I did well. A silence fell over them, and Old Ding asked who my teacher was. When I mentioned Pan's name, sighs of admiration filled the room. "Is it true?" he asked. I said it was, and his brother put his right fist into his left palm, an old-fashioned sign of respect, especially among fighters, and mumbled something to me. "He wants to become your apprentice," Old Ding translated, "and he doesn't want to wrestle anymore."

Later that night Old Ding, his two brothers and I returned

to the river. They unfastened two boats, the brothers taking one and us the other, and we started rowing downstream. "Aren't we going in the wrong direction?" I asked. "No! The big fish are downstream in the morning." "In the morning?" "Yes—why, do you want to fish now, too?" "Am I going fishing with you in the morning?" "Of course!" "Where will I be sleeping tonight?" He pointed to the bamboo roof. "Under that."

We anchored far enough downstream that the lights from the city no longer illuminated the sky. The stars and a nearly full moon shone brilliantly over our heads, and the movement of their reflections in the water told us when another boat passed in the distance. Each of our boats had a small charcoal brazier on deck and a kerosene lamp, burning faint yellow, hung from a pole off the bow. Watching the brothers prepare the boats for the night, their faces and hands glowing red, the wood of the boats a deep walnut color becoming ebony where the lamplight could not reach, all reflected in the pure black glass around us, I imagined that a magic spell had transported me into a Japanese woodblock print.

When it came time to go to sleep, Old Ding and I lay down, side by side, on a mattress of tattered army coats, using the same for blankets. The boat was narrow, so we pressed against each other, with our faces against the sides of the boat. He put out the kerosene lamp and pulled the bamboo cover back, so we could look up at the sky. Then we began talking.

"How far away is America?" When I told him, he giggled. "Bullshit—the world isn't that big!" He asked if I had ever seen the ocean, and when I said I had, he wanted to know what color it was. For some reason he thought it was yellow. He also thought Taiwan was an island off the coast of America. "Do you have robots in America that look just like people? I heard that you have them over there, but that sometimes they get angry and kill people." I explained as best I could that we have some very impressive technology in our country, but as yet no robots that cannot be distinguished from humans. He fell silent for a while, and I thought he had gone to sleep, but he had one more question: "Is the moon higher than space?" I thought about it for a long time but finally had to admit that I really didn't know. "But," I said, "did you know that we have sent men to the moon, and they have walked there?" He was quiet for a moment, then he laughed and laughed, and pulled the bamboo cover shut.

I woke up to feel tiny morning waves lapping at the side of the boat through my cheek. Old Ding woke at the same time and pulled back the bamboo cover. A heavy mist surrounded us, so thick we could barely see the other boat fifteen feet away. Without a word the three brothers prepared their long nets, dropped them into the water, then rowed apart. We waited half an hour or so, then rowed together again. We pulled the nets up, finding in them nothing but some mud and weeds. "Do you get angry if you don't catch anything?" I asked them. They laughed as if I had told a joke, then answered no, they didn't really care, but if they didn't catch much, they would be scolded by their wives.

Two hours passed, then a third boat appeared out of the thinning mist. It was the father, with an even longer net that spread out among three boats. We pulled it in, and still found nothing inside. "Even father will get scolded today!" Old Ding yelled, and they all doubled over with laughter. They folded up the net, and we started back to shore for breakfast. We rowed to a spot where seven other boats were moored, and where the fishermen's wives stood on the floodwall waiting to give them breakfast. I hid under the bamboo cover again, and when Old Ding's wife came down to the river with a container full of steamed bread and hot peppers, I jumped

out, exchanged greetings, then jumped with the container
back onto the boat. The other fishermen and their wives up
on the wall watched in numb silence as we divided up the
bread and started eating. In time I was properly introduced,
and we pulled our boat into their little cluster and shared
breakfast. When everyone had eaten, they took turns dropping their trousers, leaning off the sides of the boats and using
the river as a toilet. At the same time, Old Ding insisted that
it was time to wash up. He dipped an iron cup into the filthy
water and began splashing it on his face and neck, inviting
me to do the same. I declined, to everyone's surprise. "Don't
you wash yourself?" "Yes, but not every day. I will tomorrow." Then it came time to brush our teeth. He dipped the
cup into the water again, swished a lump of steel wood in it,
then put the steel wool in his mouth to chew on. He gargled
with a mouthful of the water, then spat it out. "Here—your
turn." I declined again, and everyone agreed that it was an
odd thing that Americans, who supposedly live in a fantastical
future-world, understand so little about personal hygiene.

Eventually I had to get back home, but they pleaded with
me to stay. "Why don't you live with us, here, on the boats?
Your hospital isn't far, you could ride your bicycle to class in
the mornings, then ride back in the afternoons. You can have
a boat to yourself, if you like." I told them it was very kind of
them to offer, but I had lots of books and things like that, too
much to fit on a boat. They answered that we could put some
money together and buy another boat just for my books. I
thanked them again but had to say no, assuring them that I
would visit them as often as I could. They looked disappointed but did not press the matter, and took me back to the
place where I had first met them. I hopped on shore, climbed
up the floodwall with my cello, and before disappearing over
it, turned to wave once more. They hadn't moved from the

spot, waiting for me to turn around, and waved back with both arms, reminding me to come look for them again.

The rest of the day I spent thinking about the night on the boat. Teacher Wei warned me that if I slipped away to live with the fishermen on their boats, she would be very angry, because she would probably have to teach my classes. That night I slept uneasily, dreaming that I had pulled my ears out to clean them and was driven by some horrible compulsion to chew them to pieces. I woke up feeling anxious, but pleased that my ears had not been spoiled, got ready for class and opened the door to leave the house. A crowd of old ladies, on their way to get breakfast from the dining hall, stood around the porch looking curiously at something on the steps. It was a large washbasin holding a fish, so big that its head and tail hung over the edges of the basin and touched the ground.

Pan Learns Script

A Runaway

Teacher Black

In a Gallery

enjoyed the time I spent with Pan very much, though I must admit I preferred the time he was teaching me wushu to the time he was teaching me how to teach him English. I remember with special clarity how close to madness I came the day he decided to learn to tell time. He managed to find a broken clock, set its hands at exactly twelve o'clock, then asked how to say what time it was. After he had repeated "It's twelve o'clock" to his satisfaction, he moved the minute hand exactly one minute forward to 12:01. "How do you say this?" he asked.

Eventually, though, it always came time to put away the recorders and clocks and ride over to the training hall, and no matter how short the lesson, it always seemed worth a lifetime of English tutoring. I felt that I could practice for him until my heart burst, and the times when it nearly did, and he smiled at me, I thought I would surely float up through the ceiling with joy and power. After each lesson he would tell me a story about his own training and eventual mastery. He was the youngest of several sons, and had lost his father when still very young. His older brothers apprenticed him to a metal worker and disapproved of his interest in martial arts, calling it a waste of time. He practiced secretly, at night, and sought out fifteen of the greatest masters in China, quickly becoming their favorite student. Year after year he forged metal during the day and practiced slavishly at night, returning home after the rest of his family had gone to bed. Not even his neighbors knew about his hobby, for Pan wanted no one to see him until he was ready. When that day came, he signed himself up for the national competition in Beijing, took a week off from his job, and without even a proper uniform or a pair of sneakers, became China's grand champion.

Several things hindered our lessons, though. One problem, of course, was that officialdom felt uneasy about our relationship. I was able, in time, to convince my college that denying me permission to see my teacher would not be "convenient" for me, but the cadres of the Sports Unit, whom I never saw, thought differently. One day during my second year, when I went there to drop off an English tape, a guard stopped me at the gate. "You can't come in here anymore," she said. "Don't ever come back." I asked the Foreign Affairs Bureau to make inquiries and find out what had gone wrong. The first message from the Sports Unit went something like this: "Chinese wushu is a National Defense Secret and as such, cannot be leaked to aliens." This was nonsense, so we asked for a better reason. The next message, that Master Pan was away on a very long trip, would have been more believable had Pan not been in my room when I heard it. By the third message, we were getting warmer. It was feared that I was a spy and might gain access to "internal documents" kept in the offices below the training hall, which contained such State Secrets as the number of athletes in the unit, their names, ages and so on. After several weeks, though, the most reasonable explanation reached our college. China was at that time undergoing a nation-wide purge of incompetent, radical leftist elements, known as the Party Rectification Campaign. This meant that cadres at all levels were subject to evaluation and were likely to be shifted around according to the results. Rumor had it that quite a bit of shifitng around had occurred within the leadership of the Sports Unit, though no one really knew for sure. Anyway, a team of new, forward-thinking moderate progressives had presumably just come to power. It might seem odd that their first step toward modernization and "Opening Up to the West" was to forbid me to pass through their gate. But China was at that time in the middle of another nation-wide movement, the Campaign for the Elimination of Cultural Pollution, "cultural pollution" meaning Western ideas and habits. The new leaders encouraged the adoption of Western management and training methods in their unit, but at the same time had to demonstrate a firm resolution to protect their unit from contamination by a Western person.

No further explanations were given, and I never saw the training hall or the athletes again. After that, Pan taught me on the roof of a public bathhouse early in the mornings, where we had to dodge wires, piles of roofing materials and gusts of steam that shot up through ventilation holes under our feet.

Time was another problem. Pan accompanied the troupe on all of their trips to perform or to compete. One of these trips took them to Shanghai for a month, another to Wuhan for three weeks, and a trip to Singapore and Hong Kong kept him away for more than two months. They often performed in neighboring counties in Hunan, which involved four to five days of preparation, and Pan occasionally had to travel by himself within the province to choose new troupe members. He never knew beforehand how long these trips would last, or whether during the trip he might suddenly be called to

Beijing or Hong Kong to make another movie. Since I could not go to his unit, I never knew when he was in town, or for how long, until he apepared at my door. I lived in constant fear of his showing up when I didn't happen to be home, and disappearing again for another few weeks, which frequently happened. Before the long trips, though, he always managed to find me and deluge me with new material, sometimes showing up on the rooftop every morning at five o'clock for weeks at a stretch. "When I come back, this should be perfect," he would say, then disappear.

As for his English, something had temporarily distracted him from memorizing the oral English "routines," and according to his wife, occupied him during nearly all his free moments. Apparently he had seen in my room a letter from a friend written in script. He was so taken by its appearance that he decided right away to learn it, even though he could not write in print yet. My protests were futile. I drew up a series of models for him to copy from, and barely escaped having to rewrite all of our phrase sheets in script as well. His wife sensed my frustration, and one night, as he sat at a little table copying out letters onto a pad that he always carried around with him, she pleaded with him to be reasonable and let me teach him the way I knew how. "After all," she groaned, "teaching English is his job." Pan's eyebrows shot up and he glared at her. "Neither of you understands me," he whispered. "No one understands me the way I do." Then he picked up a single chopstick. "In the hands of an ordinary man, this is just a chopstick." He looked at it for a moment, then burst into motion too fast to see clearly, bringing the chopstick to a trembling halt less than a centimeter from my throat. "In my hands it becomes something else. You think it is foolish that I want to write script, but I do what I like, and who knows what I will do with it? Who knows what these letters will become when they are mine to use?" His eyes burned into mine, then a boyish smile came over his face and he moved on to the next letter.

At seven o'clock I was finishing up my coffee and wondering whether to wake Bill. He almost never overslept, especially on days when he had morning class. I walked over to his bedroom door and knocked. "Just a minute," he called, then opened the door a crack. "I'll be right out. I have a visitor who isn't awake yet." I shuffled back into the common room and told the others. We looked at each other in stunned silence and waited.

A few minutes later Bill walked into the common room with his visitor—an eleven-year-old boy with thick, dark eyebrows and narrow eyes that looked at me without fear. His face was streaked with grime, his clothes looked badly worn, and his shoes were caked with mud. "He showed up here at about four-thirty," Bill said. "He got off the train in Changsha at about three in the morning, then walked here from the train station. Isn't that incredible?"

"Who is he?" Bob asked.

Bill sat down, scratched his forehead, then told us how he knew the boy. "I know this will sound unbelievable, but this is a runaway I met last year in Sichuan Province! I was climbing Emei Mountain when this kid latches onto me and asks if he can travel with me for a while. He told me he was from a village in Hunan, but that when he was about nine or so he decided he didn't like hanging around at home and took off to travel all over the world. He also told me he had two brothers and a sister, but a few hours later it became three sisters and no brothers, and the last I remember we had settled on three brothers and two sisters. He said he travels by

his wits and doesn't need money—no one ever asks him for
tickets, thinking he's just someone's kid who didn't want to
sit with his parents on the train. We stuck together for about
two days, then I had to leave. He wanted to go with me, but I
told him it was impossible. I gave him my address here,
though, and told him to write me every once in a while.
About six months ago I got a letter from him. He was home
again and said that he had talked it over with his parents and
they had agreed to let him become my adopted son! So he
asks if I will take him to America. If not, he says, could I just
send him a few hundred dollars foreign currency? I don't remember if I wrote him back or not. Anyway, I guess he's on
the road again." Bill asked the boy if he wanted some tea. The
boy shook his head. "Nope. I don't drink tea anymore. I want
coffee—that's what you foreign uncles drink, isn't it?" Bill
laughed and asked the boy if he had ever had coffee before.
"Nope. But that's what you drink, isn't it, Uncle Bill? Let me
have some of that."

"Imagine," Bill said as he poured the coffee, "in a society
like this, where there are regulations prohibiting everything
—then this eleven-year-old just decides to take off and see the
world, and no one stops him. It's like something out of a
Mark Twain story, isn't it?" The boy took a sip of the coffee
and made a face. "Bitter. Can I use the bathroom?" Bill led
him to our bathroom and showed him how to use our Western-
style toilet. When the boy came out a few minutes later, Bill
asked him, "Do other boys want to travel all over the world
like you?"

"Nope."

"Why do you, then? What makes you so different?"

The boy shrugged. "They don't have the abilities that I
do." He gulped down some more of the coffee, then sat in a
chair, his feet not quite reaching the floor.

By lunchtime most of the college knew about the little run-away living in Teacher Bill's room. Old Sheep threw a fit when she saw him, saying that he was filthy and covered with lice, making her job difficult, since she cleaned our thick cotten bedsheets. Fatty Du came over to have a look at him and asked him in a booming voice if he realized that by running away and skipping school, he was becoming stupid while all of his peers were becoming smart. The boy frowned and answered that he was smarter than any of them and didn't need to go to school. In the afternoon we were visited by Comrade Hu of the Foreign Affairs Bureau. After he interviewed the boy, Comrade Hu told us that, of course, he could not live with us any longer.

"We will provide a bed for him in the college Guest House until we find out who he is, then we will arrange to have him sent home."

"I understand that he must go home," Bill said, "but can't he stay with me until he leaves? I like him, and he certainly can't be dangerous."

Comrade Hu shook his head. "That would be impossible. According to regulations, any visitor here in the Foreign Guest Building must register with the Public Security Bureau. This boy does not have a Work Card, so he does not have a number. Without a number, he cannot register. Don't worry, we will bring him back to say goodbye before he is sent home. And now, let's go." With that he took the boy by the arm and led him away.

That night we sat in the common room and wondered what would become of him. Would he be severely punished for having shamed China by coming to our house? Foreigners are not supposed to see beggars, prostitutes or runaways, not to mention put them up for the night. Just as we got up to go to bed, the boy sauntered into the room, hands in his pockets, and sat down.

"What are you doing here?" Bill asked.

"I don't like those people," the boy said. "So I left. I would rather sleep here."

"But how did you get into our building?"

"The back door isn't quite closed. I noticed it this morning. I notice things like that. I am very clever."

The next day while Bill had class I kept the boy company, letting him join me as I gathered props for that night's lecture, "Crime and Punishment in America." Bob and Marcy were giving the lecture, but I had promised to help by dressing up as a policeman and catching Bob in the act of holding up Marcy. The boy showed great interest in the project, asking if he could go to the lecture and watch. "I like acting," he said. "I can act, you know. But I think it would be interesting to watch you foreign uncles act. I think I should learn some English, though, so I'll understand what you say tonight." I told him that one morning wasn't enough time to learn English, but that if he worked hard at it, I was sure he could learn very quickly.

"Yes, I think so. I learn very fast."

As I opened my closet to get a woolen cap for Bob to wear, the boy noticed a sabre hanging from a coat hook inside. "Uncle Bill tells me you are learning Chinese wushu. Do you learn fast, too?"

"Well, I doubt I'm as clever as you."

"Hm. I think you must be. Probably more clever than me, because you can speak Chinese and English. I can only speak Chinese. Yes, I'm sure you are more clever than me."

This bit of humility softened my attitude towards him; in truth, up until that moment I did not like the boy at all.

When I was eleven years old, I was small for my age, weak, and a shy, sniveling coward. I was forever being punched or teased by cunning, worldly boys like this one who, it seemed to me, could get away with anything. This boy's casual arrogance, and the ease with which he had become the center of attention in our house, bothered me. Maybe he sensed my coolness toward him, for he made every effort to speak politely to me.

"Could you perform some of your wushu for me? Uncle Bill says you are very hard-working, so I think your wushu must be very good." I felt myself liking the boy more and more. I showed him a routine with the sabre, and he clapped when I finished, asking very nicely if I would show him another. Just as I got started, the local gang of spoiled six to eight-year-old boys, who were a terrible nuisance, made their usual appearance. Whenever I practiced they surrounded me, yelling, poking little twigs at me, and singing "Waiguoren, waiguoren!"—foreigner, foreigner—over and over. When I tried to chase them away, they only hooted with laughter and became naughtier, challenging each other to run forward and touch my legs, and so on. Adults would walk by all the time and see this happen, but no one ever helped me by scolding the boys. Rude little boys are called "little devils" in China and are looked upon with amusement. So I usually had to interrupt my practice, go inside, and wait until they got bored and left.

When the youngsters began poking me with the twigs, I stopped and told the runaway to follow me inside for a few minutes. He grasped immediately what was going on, but instead of following me in, he marched up to the leader of the pack and delivered a forceful lecture. "Do you think it is polite to do what you have just done? He's working, and you bothered him! Don't you have any manners? Didn't your mother ever teach you how to behave? Now go home!" The boys, their eyes wide with fear and amazement, dropped their twigs and left without a murmur. In my eyes the runaway was now a hero. I did all of my wushu routines for him, made him some coffee and showed him some pictures of America.

That afternoon Comrade Hu returned. He sat us all down in the common room, then told us what he had been able to learn about the boy. "We have contacted his parents, who live in a village two days' bus ride from here. As you know, this is not the first time he has run away. His parents say that he stole a large sum of money before he left." Turning to the boy, Comrade Hu asked if he still had the money.

"Nope. I spent it."

"Do you have any money at all?"

"No."

"You will have to come with me now." Comrade Hu turned back to us and said in English, "We will put him on a bus for his village tomorrow. We are sorry for the inconvenience this has caused you." We assured Comrade Hu that the boy had been a pleasant enough guest, so we hoped that "disturbing foreigners" would not be added to his list of crimes.

That night after dinner the boy strode once again into our common room and sat down. "I'd rather sleep here again," he said. "And besides, I want to see your lecture tonight."

We took him to the lecture and he sat quietly in the back for the whole ninety minutes. Bob and Marcy stayed on afterward to answer questions, so the boy walked with me back to the house. We were making our way through the maze of gates and walls leading to our compound when he turned to me and said, "There's a shortcut, you know." "Really?" "Yes. Follow me."

He led me, in pitch-darkness, to a hole in a wall that I had never noticed before. Passing through it, we nearly halved the distance we had to walk.

"How did you know about that shortcut?" I asked, thoroughly impressed.

"I saw it this morning. I notice things like that."

Later that night Bill announced that he would take the boy to the bus station early the next morning and pay for the ticket himself. "Do you plan on running away again?" Bill asked him.

"Probably."

"I see. And where will you go next time?"

"Hong Kong."

Bill laughed in surprise. "Hong Kong? What do you know about Hong Kong?"

The boy picked his nose before answering. "It's a big department store, isn't it?"

"Not really," Bill said, reaching over and picking up the small black vinyl bag the boy always carried with him—his only luggage. "I hope you don't mind, but I think I'd better look in here." The boy didn't flinch. Bill opened it and pulled out a few postcards and bric-a-brac taken from our common room.

"Just souvenirs," the boy said. The objects were all valueless, so Bill put them back into his bag, saying, "You should never take things without asking, no matter how unimportant they are."

"Sorry."

By the time I woke up, Bill was already back from the station. "Is he gone?" I asked. "Yes, I put him on the bus. I took him out there early so I wouldn't attract attention—I could just see someone alerting the Public Security Bureau that they saw a foreigner kidnapping a Chinese boy on the back of his bicycle. Wouldn't you know it, though? I was riding over the bridge, when who should come up from the other side but the whole Public Security Bureau Academy, marching before breakfast in full uniform. Just my luck. Anyway, I got him on the bus. I made him promise, since I bought him the ticket, not to jump off it and to go home this time. He said 'Sure,' waved goodbye, then hopped on—just like that."

The boy became the topic of discussion in most of my classes for several days after that. Almost all my students agreed that the boy was a "bad element" and needed to be disciplined. One aging doctor, though, had a different opinion. She had surprised me once before in class when we talked about retirement. Many doctors in China are not allowed to retire, and some of them have never even had a vacation. This woman announced that she had a retirement plan: she would pretend to die, have herself nailed into a coffin and driven to her home village, then climb out during the funeral and declare herself a ghost. "Then I could have a garden and take care of my grandchildren." She agreed with the others that the runaway was a bad boy. "But," she said quietly, "this boy has imagination."

During the summer between my two years I returned to the States, where I practiced Pan's routines in Central Park and drank milk shakes for breakfast, lunch and dinner. While there I picked up some sheet music for a woman in Changsha, a professional singer, who had taught herself to play classical guitar and desperately wanted new material. I brought her the music in September and she vowed to repay the favor.

One week later she appeared at the medical college with a strikingly handsome man who looked about forty and who wore the coordinated outfit of a professional athlete. She stepped forward to greet me while the man stood politely behind. "This is Teacher Hei," she said. "His surname is very uncommon—it means 'black.' Most dancers and musicians in Changsha know about him because he teaches wushu in the Arts and Culture Department of Hunan Teachers' College. I don't know him personally, but many of my classmates do. They say that his wushu is very good. Even more important, though, they say he is a wonderful man. When I told him about you, he said he would be willing to assist you in your study." She led me over to him and introduced us. He smiled shyly and said, "I told the young lady several times that my wushu would not be good enough to be of use to you, but she insisted that I come anyway."

"Don't be polite," I said. "She speaks very highly of your skills." He shook his head. "My wushu is not exceptional. It will seem especially ordinary to you, who are the student of

Pan Qingfu. He is no ordinary man. Why would you need further instruction?"

"I am very fortunate to be Master Pan's student, but, you know, he leaves Changsha all the time. I get discouraged when I don't have someone to go to, who will push me to keep trying."

"I understand," he said. "I will help you in any way I can. But I must ask that you do not mention to Master Pan that you are studying with me."

"Not tell him?"

"Try to understand. He is famous in China, a well-known fighter. He has chosen to teach you, so of course many Chinese are envious of you. Some say he teaches you because you have a great desire and you work hard. But some say it is because you are a foreigner—you are his exotic pet. Master Pan takes a great risk, teaching you. If he knows that you are studying with me, he will think that you feel dissatisfied, and he will be insulted because I am so common. Please, let it be our secret."

"If you say so."

"The other thing is that I don't want you to pay me or give me any gifts—it would only cause trouble. I teach for my own pleasure. Just let me know when to expect you so I can be prepared."

"You are terribly kind, Teacher Hei, but how can I show my appreciation? I'll feel embarrassed if I can't do something for you."

He stared at me for a moment, then laughed. "Practice, of course! It sounds so easy, but so few students do. Shall we start now?" The singer, her obligation fulfilled, said goodbye, and right there on the sidewalk Hei began teaching me the footwork of the two styles he loved most, Xingyiquan and

Baguazhang. These styles are closely related, so a master of one usually becomes competent at the other as well. According to popular history, a *xingyi* master and a *bagua* master competed against each other in the last century, but when several matches held over three days produced no clear winner, they became friends and agreed that their two styles should from that time on be taught and learned together. After Hei demonstrated the fundamentals of the two styles, he performed an advanced routine of each, to give me an idea of the distinct character of the two systems. It was not difficult for me to see that his skill was by no means "common."

After an hour's lesson and a break for tea he suggested that I follow him home so I would know how to get there next time. He lived across the river on the far side of Yuelu Mountain, a fifty-minute ride that took us along a narrow, battered road jammed with overloaded trucks, homemade tractors, wheelbarrows carrying screaming pigs and buses going back and forth from the countryside. About a mile from his home, as I strained to pedal up a hill, my bicycle chain snapped. We walked it to a roadside "fix bicycle" stand; just as the repairman got over the shock of seeing me, a loud bell rang and the local elementary school across the street let out for the afternoon. A huge iron gate swung open, releasing a horde of children who perceived and then surrounded me like a single, vast organism. After an eternity the chain was fixed and we managed to ride through the sea of children. Teacher Hei, looking dazed, asked me if I always drew crowds like that when I rode my bicycle. "I'm afraid so." "Oh . . . well, you know, you are quite a spectacle. Not many people look like you around here." I asked Teacher Hei if people in Changsha thought I looked ugly. "Oh, no!"

he answered quickly. "Not ugly—you look . . . interesting! You have a very three-dimensional face."

When we reached his house, I felt as if we had left Changsha completely. He lived in a small, red-brick building surrounded by trees and terraced vegetable plots, all tucked away on the slope of Yuelu Mountain not far below an orange grove. An old man sat in the shade of a tree growing near the building, playing the *erhu*, a Chinese stringed instrument. Hei explained that this group of two-story buildings housed teachers in the Arts and Culture Department of the Teachers' College. His neighbors were painters, dancers, musicians, scholars and athletes. When we walked into his apartment, a flock of chickens that slept under his stove at night ran forward to be fed. Hei motioned for me to sit in a large chair while he sat on a low stool near a window. He stretched his arm out of the window where a young tree stood and plucked a few tiny, oval-shaped fruits off it. "Do you like kumquats?" he asked. "This tree is doing well." I had never seen a fresh kumquat; I told him I liked preserved kumquats, but had never tried them off the tree. He dropped the fruits into a tin cup filled with boiling water, poked them around for a minute, then handed me one. He watched me carefully, and when he saw how much I enjoyed it, he went outside, picked twenty more and put them into my bag. He introduced me to his wife, who quietly insisted that I try a few tea-cooked eggs that she had just prepared. Then I left, having agreed to come three afternoons a week thereafter for lessons.

When I next came I found Hei out in the terraced vegetable patch harvesting some kind of spinach. He heard the bell on my bicycle and came trotting down the hill, his shoulder pole bent with the weight of two buckets full of nightsoil, which he used as fertilizer. A cup of tea that he had steeped earlier and let cool waited for me inside; he knew I liked "cold drinks." After I finished it he cleaned a few kumquats for me, watched me eat them, then took me outside to practice. During the lesson I heard a piano through the window above Teacher Hei's apartment. The playing was beautiful, and it complemented the calm grace of Hei's movements. He stepped, turned, parried and struck in rapid, gentle circles. Unlike Pan's eyes, which flashed with exquisite violence, Hei's eyes looked alert but expressionless, almost like a bird's. His first criticism of my attempt to learn the straight punch of xingyi was that my shoulders and arms were too tense. "Even your hands should relax," he said, "tensing and snapping only at the moment of impact." He took my hand in his to show me the correct posture and noticed the scars on my knuckles. "You are hitting iron, I see." I looked at his hands and saw that they were unmarked. "Teacher Hei, do you condition your hands in any way?" He spread his hands in front of him and looked at them as if trying to decide something. "No, I don't. I suppose I could, but in truth, I can't think of a good reason for it. What would I do with such powerful hands? I'm a college teacher and a gardener, not a warrior. Besides, the wushu I practice does not require it. When you practice, your hands should look fluid and graceful, as if they were made of silk. They become hard only for an instant, like the end of a whip as it cracks, then they are soft again."

Hei went into the house for a few minutes to check on the stew he was cooking, leaving me outside to practice the straight punch. An old woman wearing a plain white blouse and a grey skirt appeared in one of the doorways and sat down on a stool to watch me. I smiled at her and she smiled back, waving at me and gesturing for me to continue. I kept it up for a while, then paused to stand in the shade of a tree. "I think it's wonderful that you are making such good use of your time here in China," the old woman said all of a sudden. "Your teacher says you are an exceptionally diligent student."

"Well, it's very nice of him to—" I stopped in mid-sentence and blinked. She had complimented me in fluent English. "You-you speak English!"

"Why yes, I do. I grew up in the States. I imagine that was some time before you were born."

"And—now you live here, in Changsha?"

"That's right. I live right upstairs. That was my piano you must have heard. I'm a piano teacher here. You see, I was a piano student in the forties. I was visiting China at the time of the Revolution. Of course, it became difficult to enter or leave China at that time, so . . . now I live here."

I didn't know what to say. She stood up, brushing her skirt daintily, then walked over to where I was standing. "You're lucky to have a teacher like Mr. Hei. He is a kind and generous man. Do you see all the gardens and trees around here? He planted them all. He dug all those terraces, too. And he shares what he grows with the whole neighborhood. Everyone likes him, because he is a real gentleman. He is out of the house every morning at four o'clock to exercise, then at five he rides across the river to teach wushu in the park. He does it for free, you know! Really, there are so few people like him." Just then Teacher Hei came out of the house. The old woman said to me, "Back to work, now! Come visit me whenever you like—I have some instant coffee that a relative sent, so I could make you a cup if you like." She waved goodbye and disappeared into the building. "So that's what English sounds like," Teacher Hei said, then he asked me how my straight punch was coming along.

By wintertime I was getting fairly comfortable with

Teacher Hei's xingyi and bagua. My biggest problem, he said, was still the same: I did not relax enough. He had thought it over and decided that if I was serious about learning soft-style boxing, I should study Taijiquan, the quintessential "soft" martial art. "My Taijiquan is not good enough, but I know someone who is very good. If you like, I will approach him and ask if he will teach you."

One week later Teacher Hei took me to a small old house in the center of the city, with a ceiling of exposed wood, stained black from the accumulated smoke of incense and coal. There he introduced me to Teacher Yi, who was in his forties, and to Yi's father-in-law, Old Zai, who was in his eighties. Both of them were well-known *taiji* experts in Changsha; Yi was chairman of the city-wide wushu association. They practiced the Wu style of taiji, native to Changsha, distinctive for its method of leaning with the whole upper body in the direction of attack rather than maintaining a strictly upright posture. They taught their students right there in the house, in an area no larger than fifteen by eight feet. As we talked, two advanced students practiced "push hands," a kind of sparring that moves slowly and gently until one partner senses the other losing his balance and takes advantage of it instantly, sending his opponent flying with a well-timed push. They had cigarettes in their mouths as they fought: the cigarette and incense smoke was so thick they looked like figures in a hazy dreamscape, writhing and bobbing like serpents, then suddenly bursting apart with one left standing and the other crashing into a wall and sliding down to the floor. "Teacher Hei has asked me to teach you taiji," Yi said at last. "Usually I wouldn't consider it, because you will only be here a short time. My father and I only accept students who are willing to study for at least five years.

Even that is only a beginning! Teacher Hei is my friend, though, and he thinks it would be worthwhile, so why don't you come three nights a week, starting next week. I would like you to come here early Sunday morning for the first lesson."

When I arrived that Sunday, instead of taking me into the house he told me to get back on my bicycle and follow him. We rode to the home of a young man, another beginning student, who joined us on our way across the river to Yuelu Mountain. We hiked to an old Taoist temple halfway up, where a young man sitting by the entrance greeted us. He led us into a sitting room and served us tea and cookies. I noticed something strange about the way he moved; when he stepped out of the room, Yi told me the boy was blind. "His taiji is coming along nicely, though." After our snack the three of us said goodbye to the young man and climbed to a clearing near the top, from which we had a view of the river. There, Yi told us to sit down and watch him practice the form, which took almost thirty minutes. He practiced it so slowly I sometimes thought he had stopped moving, but even so it seemed that his clothes would burst from the strength underneath. After that he taught us the first move of the form. "It's important to get off to a good start," Yi said. "This is the right kind of atmosphere. In the future, when you practice at my house or anywhere else, if you find your mind getting cluttered, close your eyes and remember this scene."

On a pretty day between the cold rains of winter and the steaming rains of spring, Hei and I took a pair of spears up the mountain to a clearing by an orange grove. We weren't the only ones to think of this—a few minutes after we got there, a teacher of traditional Chinese dance brought five of her apprentices to the same clearing. At first the girls, all in their mid-teens, hid their faces in their hands with embarrassment, unable to concentrate with me only a few yards away. Gradually they settled down, though, and began their dance. The older woman sang while the girls, all petite and moon-faced, danced with silk handkerchiefs in their hands. The handkerchiefs seemed to come to life in the air, floating and darting around the girls like birds. "Do you remember when I told you that your hands should move as if they were made of silk?" Hei asked me. "Yes." "Well, that's what I mean. Isn't it beautiful?" Somehow this seemed a good time to ask a question that had been nagging me for some time. "Teacher Hei, I have a question." "Mm?" "Sometimes I get confused —I don't understand why I spend so much time learning wushu. I'm not a fighter—I've never been in a fight in my life—so what am I doing this for?"

Hei thought for a while, never taking his eyes off the dancers. Then he said, "You don't have to be a fighter to enjoy wushu. If you were really training for combat, you wouldn't practice wushu. You would become a soldier." He pointed to the spear I was holding. "Look at this thing. Do you really think it has any practical use in this century? Can you carry it with you in case of attack and still feel like a respectable man? It is a cultural artifact now, not a weapon. But should we throw away all our spears and all the skill developed for them? I don't think so. It would seem like a waste to me."

"I guess I see what you mean, but still, what reason can I give myself for all this effort?" Teacher Hei shrugged his shoulders, then answered, "I don't know—why dance with handkerchiefs?"

.   .   .

"I think the taiji is helping," Teacher Hei said one afternoon. "You look more relaxed. That solves one problem. You have another problem, though, and it doesn't have anything to do with martial arts. You don't dress warmly enough! You wear a heavy army coat when you ride here, but the ride gets you all sweaty, so you take it off as soon as you arrive. That way you get a chill! You don't wear the proper clothing for the Hunan climate. Again I have called upon an expert to help you—my wife. She believes she can solve the problem." He called her from outside, where she was washing clothes. She walked over to a closet and pulled out a beautiful jet-black turtleneck sweater. It was made of thick, heavy wool. I tried it on and it fit perfectly. "She knitted it herself," Teacher Hei said proudly, "guessing your size just by looking at you." I groped for the appropriate words to thank her but she interrupted me. "It's black. That way, when you leave us, you can remember your Teacher Black." She blushed, then hurried back outside to finish her laundry.

It had been one thing after another the day I stabbed myself with the sword. Several of my students had been completely unprepared for class, I had ridden across the river for a wushu lesson but Teacher Hei was not at home, and when I got back and started practicing I strained a hamstring within half an hour. I limped through most of my routines, saving the one I was studying at the time, the Drunken Sword, for last. This technique was created some time ago by the student of a famous swordsman, who one day gave up in despair, thinking he could never progress beyond the stage he had reached. He left his master's house, supposedly for good, and went directly to a wineshop in the nearby village. There he got drunk. As he staggered out he was confronted by his teacher, who threw a wooden sword at him in disgust and told him to prepare for a good beating. The student, relaxed and made bold by the wine, gave the master a good beating instead—in front of all the other students, no less. The next day apologies were made and all was forgiven, but all was not forgotten; the students who witnessed the fight went away to the wineshop and began their study of this new method.

My routine called for me to leap, spin in the air and land in a twisted posture. I remember thinking in mid-air that I had not jumped high enough to land properly. When I hit the ground I felt a blinding pain and looked down to see that I had sent the tip of the thirty-six inch blade into my thigh. Thankful that my aim had not been worse, I pulled it out, dressed the wound and decided to go shopping to cheer myself up.

In all my time in China I had never treated myself to anything but sweatsuits and wushu equipment, so that day I decided to buy a painting. I went to a painting and calligraphy gallery that Hai Bin had recommended, a huge room on the second floor of the Hunan Museum annex, and started to browse. There were only two other people in the room, a sales clerk and an older Chinese man who appeared to be dozing in a large padded chair. The sales clerk walked over, took my arm and led me away from the "boring" monochrome paintings I was looking at, to a section of the room that had a sign, "Welcome Foreign Friends," taped on one wall. There hung several dozen colorful portraits of Chinese minority women with tiny waists and enormous breasts, dressed in alluring "native costumes," gathering berries or drawing water from rustic wells. Even if I had wanted one of these monstrosities I could not have afforded it, so I told the clerk I preferred the "boring" monochromes and returned to that part of the gallery. The old man in the chair had apparently listened to our conversation, for he got up, walked over to a few feet from where I stood and silently watched me as I looked at the paintings. "You speak Chinese," he said at last. "Yes, a little bit." He lit a cigarette, leaned his head to one side and squinted. "That's incredible." "Not really," I replied. "I live here, I have to speak Chinese." "You live here?" he asked, his eyes opening up. "Yes—I teach at the medical college." He flicked the ashes of his cigarette, shaking his head. "That's incredible."

He was quiet for a few minutes, then asked, "So you don't like the girlie paintings, huh?" "No, do you?" He broke into a smile. "I'm Chinese! How can I like that kind of thing?

That's for foreigners. But you're a foreigner and you don't like them. What do you like?" I pointed to my favorite piece, a small ink painting of three shrimp. "And why do you like it?" he asked. "Because it's simple," I answered. We compared a few paintings and a few pieces of calligraphy, then he asked me to follow him downstairs for a moment. At the bottom of the stairs he pointed to a large mural depicting a mist-shrouded valley filled with soldiers, jeeps, trucks, smokestacks, utility poles and television antennas. "What do you think?" I told him I didn't like it. "Why not?" he asked, narrowing his eyes. "Too many jeeps," I answered, and he laughed, grasped my hand and shook it for some time. "I'll have you know I painted that mural," he said, "and you're exactly right! There are too many jeeps in it! You don't know how wonderful it is to hear someone say that! Just for saying that, I'm going to paint you a landscape, I promise you!" He wrote down his address and told me to visit him a week later, after xiuxi.

When I got there, his whole family greeted me and fed me all sorts of nuts, sunflower seeds, dried beans and tea. The artist, Master Lu, took out a photo album showing pictures of favorite works he had sold. He turned out to be one of the best-known painters in Hunan, who was frequently commissioned by the State to paint murals for important halls and smaller paintings for visiting dignitaries. Finally, after clearing a space on the wall, he took a freshly mounted scroll from his desk. He carefully unrolled it, hung it from a nail high up on the wall, then stood back to let me see it. It was an imaginary scene in the mountains with no sign of industrialization in sight, inscribed with a poem in a style of calligraphy he had seen me admiring in the art gallery. Master Lu sat back in his chair, drew on his cigarette and squinted at the painting. "No jeeps. Just mountains."

Unsuitable Reading

No Sad, No Cry

Thinning Hair

Bad Elements

On October 1, China's National Day, the Provincial Foreign Affairs Bureau arranged a banquet for all the foreigners living and working in Hunan. Prior to the banquet our host, a high official within the Provincial Government, held a meeting at which he gave us a "brief review of current political, economic and social issues affecting the province." This brief review, translated a sentence at a time into English, turned out to be a very lengthy recitation of statistics, all showing remarkable growth, interspersed with firm declarations of purpose, goals for the year 2000 and conclusive evidence that these goals would be met. The official sat completely still as he delivered this speech, moving his lips only as much as he had to except at the end of paragraphs, when he pulled them open to smile, shaking his head from side to side so that the smile fell upon all members of the audience equally.

After two hours the translator showed signs of fatigue. Something about striving from victory to victory was translated as "And the broad collective masses, by means of the leadership of the Chinese Communist Party, and under the protection of the new Constitution approved during the Twelfth Party Congress, shall—shall strike from factory to factory in order to realize the goals of the Four Modernizations by the year 2000." By the third hour, the poor translator had become delirious, stumbling over nearly every sentence.

No one experienced fatigue more than the audience, however, for of the fifty foreigners there, about ten spoke both English and Chinese, whereas the rest, from Japan and Romania, understood neither English nor Chinese.

In the room sat an almost equal number of Chinese, mostly Foreign Affairs representatives, some local government bureaucrats and translators from the institutions with foreign expert programs. Watching them, I could understand why they do not appreciate the Westerner's irritation with long, boring meetings. The Chinese have, by necessity, increased their endurance manyfold by making listening optional. During meetings they talk with one another, doze, get up to stretch or walk around, and in general do not pretend to pay attention. This does not seem to offend the speaker, who, in general, does not pretend to be interested in what he or she is saying.

A Chinese man sitting next to me had been dozing quite freely since the first hour of the speech. He opened his eyes during the third hour to reach for his teacup, and noticed me looking at him. He had extremely thick glasses, a bloated face and a few beads of sweat on his forehead that he wiped at with a dirty handkerchief. He stared at me with no expression on his face for a long time, then suddenly asked me what I thought of the meeting. I said I thought it was very boring, too long and repetitious. His face did not change at all and he continued to stare at me. "That is because you are listening," he said, and went back to sleep.

I happened to see this man again on several occasions, and each time talked with him at greater length. Though extremely shy at first, he eventually loosened up and spoke freely about his interests and ambitions. In time I found him to be a very warm person, and despite his stiff, expressionless manner, he had a sense of humor as well. No matter how funny something was, however, he always told or heard it with that deadpan face, wiping at his forehead and staring at me from behind his colossal lenses.

Some time later he came to my house to talk about a project that he wanted help with. He translated Western novels into Chinese in his spare time and hoped one day to publish. The problem was that, like most Chinese, he had no access to recent works—meaning nearly everything published since 1930. He wondered if I could lend him some contemporary American novels that might be suitable for translation. I said that he could borrow as many as he liked from my bookcase, and that if he had anything specific in mind, I would try to get it for him. He didn't seem to have anything specific in mind, so I let him take a few books at random and asked that he return them by the end of the year.

To my surprise he returned a few weeks later, having read all of them. He put them carefully back into the bookcase, exactly where they had been before, and stared at me. "How did you like them?" I asked. Without blinking he replied, "Thank you very much, but I'm afraid these books would be unsuitable for publication in China. They contain scenes and language that would be considered decadent, or even pornographic." I said that I was sorry to hear that, and tried to think of books I had that might be more suitable. I chose a few short story collections and told him to read through them. "Even though these aren't novels, they are examples of recent American literature, and since this is a high school English textbook, I doubt they contain much pornography." He thanked me again and left.

A month or so later he returned, and once again put the

books very carefully back into the bookcase. He wiped his forehead and apologized for keeping the books so long. "I'm afraid that these stories are also unsuitable for publication in China. They have heroes who represent pessimism, alienation and individualism, all of which, as you know, are considered detrimental to the cause of Socialism. Do you have anything else?" I had to admit, with some irritation, that I could think of no books in my possession that would be considered beneficial to the cause of Socialism. "I understand," he said, and began to leave. Passing by the bookshelf he noticed a large book that had not been there before. It was *The World According to Garp*. He asked what it was about, and I laughed and said he should read it and find out. He took it down, put it in his bag and said he would.

Several months passed. One day I found him sitting stiffly on a chair in my room; Old Sheep had seen him waiting and put him in my room while I taught class. After saying hello he took the book from his bag and apologized for keeping it so long. "It contained many words not found in most dictionaries," he said, "and was long to begin with." I asked him what he thought of it, noticing that he was not putting it back in the bookcase as he usually did. He looked at it, seemed to think for a few moments, then stared at me. "This book," he began, "is very, very unsuitable." He paused, then went on. "In fact, in my whole life, I have never read or even imagined something so unsuitable." Here he stopped, still staring at me. He held the book up slightly and pointed at it with his chin. "May I keep it?"

Most of my teaching hours the second year were spent with a group known as the 1983 English Medical Class. This group of first-year medical students, ranging in age from seventeen to twenty, were chosen from among hundreds of talented freshmen for their superior performance on a series of English tests. They were to spend their entire first year studying English, then the remainder of their medical education was to be taught in English by doctors and teachers in our college who could speak it. Although medical schools all over China were offering rudimentary English classes to their students, our college was one of the few to set up a comprehensive English-language medical course. Controversy surrounded this program; on the one hand, the current "Open Door" policy promoted learning from the West, but on the other hand, conducting science classes in English implied that China could not really modernize on its own, with only cosmetic assistance from Western technology. Furthermore, most members of the faculty and administration of our college with the foresight to support this program had had that foresight before official policy supported it, and had been criticized or punished for it. Understandably, the program created all sorts of pressures for those involved with it.

These pressures inevitably fell on the shoulders of the thirty students of each English Medical Class—my group was the third. For days before their classes actually began, they had to endure marathon lectures by political cadres who warned them that ". . . the college, the Party, and the whole country" depended on them to succeed. Success in this case meant that they were to become fluent in English, get higher marks in their regular medical exams than other students to prove that they were not slacking off, excel in their political study to show that they did not lose sight of the Socialist Spirit, and above all, display model personal behavior at all times to show that their contact with Westerners had not "corrupted" them.

The first time I saw them I had to sit in front of the class while one of the Chinese teachers gave them a long speech about behaving well, entitled "The Twelve Be's, the Twelve Don't Be's, the Eight Do's and the Eight Don't Do's." After forty-five minutes of this he at last introduced Jan, my co-teacher for the year, and me. Jan and I stood up and said hello, but there was no response. We faced a mass of trembling paralysis.

Miraculously, though, some of them loosened up after a few weeks. Once they got over the shock and fear of being called on individually rather that reciting together as a group, classes became more interesting. Personalities began to emerge and some of the students even dared to experiment with imagination and humor. Naturally, this led to trouble. One day Teacher Wu brought Terry Lautz, the Yale-China Field Staff Director visiting that week from Hong Kong, to observe our class. The students became nervous right away, so I called on the most confident boy, whom I had given the English name Lenny, hoping that he would get things going. True to form, when I asked him what he would like to do today, he stood up, smiled and answered, "Today I would like to eat your heart and drink your blood." Everyone got excited after that, and we ended up having an energetic lesson. When the bell rang, I walked over to Teacher Wu and Terry and asked, "Aren't they a good group?" Terry, who well understood how dreary English classes in China can be, said he'd had a delightful time and complimented Teacher Wu on the quality of the students' English. Teacher Wu, looking distinctly pale, said "Mm," and called me into her office.

"What did that boy say?" she asked, horrified. "You mean Lenny? Oh, he said he wanted to eat my heart and drink my blood! Isn't he something?" Her face turned dark. "That's what I thought he said. He must be punished severely! The Field Staff Director must be furious! Think of the report he will give to your Leaders! What a horrible thing to say! You can't speak like that to a teacher! And the other students laughed! They must all be severely criticized!" I tried to convince Teacher Wu that Lenny's comment and the other students' laughter did not reflect disrespect at all, but demonstrated how perceptive they all were. "And how do you figure that?" she asked. "Because, Teacher Wu, in a very short time they have noticed that American teachers have different expectations from Chinese teachers. We like some humor and laughter in our classes, and we enjoy it if the students can occasionally joke with the teacher. The students have never insulted us. If they spoke that way to their Chinese teachers, perhaps you might criticize them, but I don't think they do. How can you criticize them for acting the way Jan and I encourage them to?" "Mm. This is terrible. If they ever spoke like that to a Chinese teacher, can you imagine what would happen to all of us? They must be criticized—this is China, and they are Chinese students." Classes were noticeably quieter for a few days after that, but in time the incident blew over and laughter returned to our classroom.

One of the greatest challenges of teaching English in China was breaking students of their compulsion to learn everything by rote and getting them to learn English by using it, instead. My favorite method was to divide them into small groups, each of which had to prepare or improvise short skits based on a given situation. At first this went very slowly. "Julian, you are a policeman. Sinbad, you are a criminal and Julian has just caught you. Have a conversation on the way to the police station." Silence. "Come on, don't be nervous. You can think of something—Julian, you start."

JULIAN: "You are a criminal."

SINBAD: "I'm sorry."

Silence. "Sinbad, why don't you try to bribe Julian?"

SINBAD: "Do you want some money?"

JULIAN: "No, thank you."

With practice, however, they became quite good at this. One assignment was to interview a Martian who had just landed on Earth and to ask him about his first impressions and so on. A pair of boys had the Martian flee to Earth to seek political asylum. He was a Communist and had been condemned to death by the ruling Fascist Bourgeois Oppressors on Mars. He hoped that the Earthlings would help him by setting him up with a human girl—if he got married he would be safe, for on Mars, he explained, there is a strict law against making widows.

Another assignment was to come up with a convincing advertisement for a product, then perform it as a television commercial. Three girls walked to the front of the classroom, all with their heads hung low. One said "I'm unhappy. I'm very fat." The second shook her head and said, "I'm unhappy, too. I'm too skinny." The third blushed, giggled, faced the blackboard and said, "I'm unhappy, too. I can't find a husband." Suddenly Juliet—she had chosen her English name after hearing my Romeo and Juliet lecture—marched to the front of the classroom with a basket filled with rolled up pieces of paper. (The students, of course, all knew that in China it is customary at weddings for the bride and groom to distribute "Happiness Candy"—any candy, preferably with the character known as "Double Happiness" printed on the wrapping—to all of their relatives and friends.) Adopting a television announcer's huge smile and enthusiastic voice, she said, "Ladies and Gentlemen! I am pleased to tell you about a wonderful thing! It is called Juliet's Happiness Candy, and it is the most wonderful thing in the world! You must have it—you must buy it today. Let me tell you about it, please. This candy makes wishes come true. If you are too fat and you eat it, you will become skinny. If you are too skinny and you eat it, you will become fat. If you are lonely, it will help you get married. Truly it solves all of your problems. Guaranteed—no sad, no cry." The three sad-looking girls ran to the desk and asked if Juliet's Happiness Candy could solve their problems. "Of course it can," Juliet assured them, "but you must buy it first."

There was one student, however, who did not seem to be adjusting. April came from a village in the Hunan countryside and had never seen Changsha before coming to college, much less a pair of American teachers. At the beginning of the semester she was so frightened she did not dare even to look up from her desk—she buried her head in her hands and would not respond to questions, and once or twice I saw tears drop onto her desk as she struggled to overcome her embarrassment. On the first quiz she did not even raise her pencil. The English Department came very close to removing her from the program and giving her place to someone less talented but more sturdy. Somehow, though, she managed to stay in the class.

Months passed before I could get her to speak audibly in class, but even then she would not look up from her desk.

On a class outing, when I took out my camera to take a picture of the group, April disappeared and hid behind a tree, too shy to be photographed. Her classmates liked her and helped her by giving her parts in skits that allowed her to remain seated. Outside of class some of the girls told me that in the dormitory April was less shy, even playful, but in the classroom she became too nervous to speak. The first time April actually raised her voice loud enough for everyone to hear, the class applauded. April curled up into a ball, covered her head with her arms and did not come up for several minutes. I thought she was crying but Juliet, who sat next to her, said, "Don't worry, Teacher Mark. April is happy—she is smiling!" I said, "April, is that true?" and though she did not say anything, her shoulders moved up and down in a little nod.

By the end of the first semester, Jan and I decided that it was time for April to sink or swim. Part of the final examination was an oral quiz. Originally we had planned to let Jan quiz April, because April was less frightened of her. But this seemed a good opportunity to force April to get over her fear. I announced in class the names of those who would test with Jan and those who would test with me, and when I said, "And April, you will be tested by me," the whole class gasped. April, though I could not see her face, appeared to stiffen.

For days before the exam the students whispered and made predictions about April's interview with Teacher Mark. A few of the girls even came to my office to ask for a change of decision on April's behalf. On the day of the exam the students waited in one room while Jan and I conducted the interviews in two other rooms. When I walked into the waiting room and called April's name, the room fell silent and everyone looked at her. April did not move. "Go into your office," Juliet said, "she will come." I went into the office and waited. Suddenly the door opened; April closed it behind her, marched up to me, looked me square in the eyes and said in a booming voice, "I'm ready!" She tested without any difficulty, and when it was over I laughed and said, "April, that was wonderful! How did you do it?" "Am I done?" she asked, still looking directly at me. "Yes, you are, and you did very well." "I know," she boomed, then shot out of the classroom, running all the way to the dormitory.

"Little Guo had another accident today," Hai Bin said as we walked to the post office one afternoon. "We were performing an experiment with a lab dog which involved a minor operation. Little Guo administered the anaesthesia. He inserted the needle, but all of a sudden used too much force. The needle entered the chest cavity and pierced the dog's heart! My advisor was very angry with Little Guo. By the way," he continued, "I think Little Guo has found another teacher for you."

Hai Bin was right; that night Little Guo appeared at the house with a short, stocky fellow who wore a blue cap. I invited them in and poured some tea. I noticed as I handed the cup to the man that the fingers on his right hand were stained a deep yellow from smoking crude cigarettes. "This is Master Liang," Little Guo said. "Master Liang doesn't talk much." As if to show me what he meant, Little Guo stopped speaking and looked at Master Liang, who indeed said nothing. After a long pause Little Guo continued: "Master Liang is a taiji expert. He is especially good at push-hands. He is the champion of Hunan Province! I met him last week and asked if he would teach you. He said he would." I smiled at Liang and thanked him. He didn't look up or smile, saying only "Mm," and drawing deeply at his cigarette. Nothing was said for several minutes, and I began to feel uncomfortable. I went to my desk and pulled out an album of photographs of my family to show him. He looked at them, nodding every once in a while or saying "Mm," but I did not get much of

a response out of him. Then he stood up. He turned to Little
Guo and said, "We should meet two or three nights a week.
Do you have a place?" Little Guo said that he knew a place
we could use. "Let's go then," Liang said, and we left my
room.

I followed them reluctantly; my impression of Master
Liang was not overwhelmingly positive, and the memory of
how sticky it had been discontinuing lessons with Zheng was
still fresh in my mind. When we reached the area Little Guo
had in mind, though—an empty basketball court—Liang
suddenly came to life. He said that taiji was an exercise of
both mind and body which, if practiced correctly, not only
improved one's health but actually halted the aging process.
Of course, he added, one way taiji prolonged life was by
increasing one's chances of survival if attacked. He demonstrated the form he thought I should learn, Chen style taiji,
distinctive for its sudden bursts of speed and power, then
asked me to push hands with him. "If you beat me," he said
with a grin, "then you will be my teacher! If I beat you, then
I will be your teacher!" He defeated me thoroughly, and
with such ease and good humor that at last I could not continue for I had to catch my breath from laughing. At one
point when I tried to throw him off balance he tickled me
under the arms. When I jumped, he rushed in low, grabbed
me by the waist and lifted me straight into the air, holding
me over his head in a clean military press. This feat of
strength became understandable when he took his shirt off
later, revealing an astounding musculature that simply could
not have been developed by practicing taiji. He grinned like
a little boy and admitted that when he was in his twenties he
had been a champion weightlifter with the Provincial Sports
Team. Nowadays he loaded hundred-pound bags of rice onto

trucks to keep in shape. "That tickle move is pretty useful," he said, suddenly becoming serious, "but it isn't a good idea if you're practicing with female comrades."

Liang turned out to be such a cheerful man that I later wondered why he had seemed so grouchy the first time we met. "Teacher Liang, why were you so quiet that night? Were you angry?"

"Angry? Are you joking? I was nervous! I'd never seen a foreigner up close before. But once we got outside where it was dark, you didn't look so frightening."

"Do I look frightening?"

"Well, your eyes maybe. . . . They are so bright, as if there were lights inside At first it was hard to look at you and talk at the same time, because whenever I saw the eyes, I forgot what I was going to say."

Liang had studied taiji with several teachers, but gained most of his expertise in a less conventional way. For many years he went out to the parks each morning, approached anyone practicing taiji and asked them to push hands with him. "For the first five years or so I lost every bout. I went home and wrote down in a little notebook how and why I lost, and studied my notes every evening. Then I started to win sometimes. I wrote down how and why I won and studied my notes every evening. I kept this up until I won every time. This is a good way to learn, but it is also the hard way. Not all boxers are good people. Many people I practiced with used unfair techniques, like kneeing me in the groin, poking at my throat, or spitting in my eyes to gain an advantage. That is not good taiji; if you can't win by legitimate technique, using the opponent's force and balance to defeat him, then you are not a good taiji player."

"What did you do when people cheated that way?" I asked.

He laughed dryly. "I criticized them, then we continued. If they did it again, I squeezed them until they fainted."

One night after dinner with his family, we took a long walk to a park and practiced there. I had been pushing hands with him for several months by then, and had still not been able to shove him off balance even once. Before we began, I warned him that tonight I would topple him no matter what. He smiled and wished me luck. Perhaps because the dinner had been so much fun, with plenty of joking and teasing back and forth, or maybe because each of us had had a glass of baijiu, we both felt especially playful that night. After a few rounds of pushing, all of which ended with me flying through the air as usual, I decided to make my move. Using all my strength I rushed forward, grabbed his arms, threw my shoulder into his chest and let loose. We locked, and for a few long seconds grappled like bears. Just as I thought I would collapse from exhaustion, I stuck my knee behind his and swept his foot out from under him. He didn't expect that, and started to go down, but as he fell he pivoted and jerked me towards him with unbelievable strength, carrying us both down to the ground with a loud thump. I hit the ground first; he had still won. We lay there tangled up for a while, gasping for breath and laughing. "Not bad!" he said, "I'll have to call you 'Little Tiger' from now on. Would that be all right?" "That would be fine, Teacher Liang. Shall I call you 'Big Tiger,' then?" "That would be wonderful! Soon the Little Tiger will be stronger than the Big Tiger, and will eat him up!" "I doubt that." We retired to a park bench to rest, watching some fireflies hover around a bamboo thicket. "What a shame you can't stay here," he said suddenly. "Then we could wrestle like this for years and years."

"I'm sure I'll come back to visit someday."

"Really? You know, there is supposed to be an international push-hands competition in China in 1986 or '87—maybe I'll see you there! Maybe you and I will have to fight for the gold medal!"

"Wouldn't that be something!"

"Oh, that would be exciting. You know, if you keep practicing taiji, you'll look the same in 1987 as you look now. Taiji keeps you young. That's why I have two daughters almost as old as you, but I have the body of a twenty-year-old."

One beautiful Sunday morning I went to Liang's house to take some pictures of him and his family. They were all dressed in brightly colored outfits, since these would be their first color photographs. Liang and his wife argued for a few minutes about something, then Liang reluctantly took off his blue cap. I realized then that I had never seen him without it. They posed in various combinations in front of their apartment; then I suggested taking a picture of Liang with his shirt off. "That way, Teacher Liang, my friends in America will believe me when I tell them how strong you are." He politely declined, at the same time unbuttoning his shirt. "Well, if you insist," he said, undoing the last button.

After I had taken the picture, he took me aside and asked in a whisper, "Could you do me a favor? Taiji has kept me young except for my hair—I'm starting to get bald. In America, people say, everything is modernized. Do you have ways of adding hair in photographs? If you could do that for me, I'd be very grateful."

The train came to a screeching, steaming halt at a mud-brick shed with a thatched roof and a forty-watt bulb hanging outside. It was a small station, but at least fifty peasants stood waiting on the platform, bent under the weight of their shoulder poles and heaping baskets. The passengers groaned when the doors opened and the peasants struggled to get on; already people were nearly faint from the heat and the crowding. As we got under way again, the men around me seemed to agree all at once to try to shift from a standing to a sitting position. We slid down, our backs against the walls, shoulders pressed together, and came to rest in a squat. I found myself knee to knee with the two young men opposite me. I hadn't noticed them before—perhaps they had gotten on at the last stop—but one of them started to talk to me as if picking up where our last conversation had left off.

They both wore battered army fatigues, had sweat and dust smeared across their faces, and reeked of baijiu. One of them was tall and broad-shouldered and looked dazed, his mouth slightly open and his bloodshot eyes staring a little past me into the wall of the train. He didn't say much. The talkative one was small and lean, and obviously the more clever of the two. His eyes darted, and his hands made all sorts of gestures as he talked, occasionally finding their way into the canvas sack where he had his bottle of baijiu. He offered me some but I refused, saying I could not drink on an empty stomach. Usually when I rode the trains I pretended not to speak or understand Chinese, because once I opened my mouth I was obliged to amuse everyone on the train by answering questions about my nationality, height, weight, age and salary—attention I enjoyed less the longer I spent in China. It was different with these two, though. They did not seem particularly impressed by me, as if they had something more exciting to think about than a Caucasian on a local train. Their casual manner disarmed me and made me curious to know what could possibly be on their minds, that they would not be impressed by me and want to know my salary.

As the shorter man got redder in the face from the baijiu, his voice got louder and his hands moved more. He told me that he and his friend had that very day been released from "corrective labor," where they had done time for having stabbed someone over a poker game.

"My friend here," he said, poking the taller man, "held the guy like this. And I took the knife and stuck it in him here, under the ribs!" He seemed to relish telling the story, making me suddenly nervous about sitting so close to him, but then he closed his eyes and smiled.

"And now we are going home! My mom will be at the station—she visited me a few times at the prison. She loves me!"

He took another shot of liquor, then closed his eyes again.

"My mom will be standing there at the station, because she loves me! When I was at the prison, she missed me and brought me home-cooked foods sometimes, and—"

The big fellow struck him hard in the chest with the back of his forearm, knocking him out of his reverie and nearly out of breath.

"What did you do that for?" the smaller man screamed, his face now crimson.

His partner looked down at the floor between his legs and said quietly, "Don't talk like that, about seeing your mom."

"Why not?"

He pointed at me without raising his eyes. "Because he's from far away. He can't see his mom at all. He doesn't need to know how happy you are."

"Don't You Know It's Snowing Out?"

A Coffee Shop

Professor Jin

After one of Pan's long trips abroad, I noticed that he looked thinner in the face and had developed a habit of pressing his left hand to his stomach and chest when he sat down. I asked him about it, but he seemed unconcerned, saying that he perhaps worried too much, but that was all. One morning, while I was riding to class, one of my doctor students called to me from a window in the hospital. She said that my teacher had collapsed and had arrived by ambulance not long before. She told me to come see him after class, that by then it would be all right to visit, then closed the window.

The two hours passed slowly. At last the class ended, and I ran over to the hospital to see Pan. By the time I got there, though, he had already left. Several nurses stood nearby talking about him, so I asked them what the problem was. They said it wasn't clear, but that he was a very interesting patient. They said the doctors wanted to keep him in the hospital for observation, but that as soon as he could stand he left, saying he had better things to do than lie around in a hospital. Even more interesting, they said, was that when one of the nurses tried to insert an intravenous device in his wrist, he wouldn't let her, saying that he needed the use of his hands just then, as he didn't want his time in the hospital to be a complete waste. He had a little pad of paper and a pen, and seemed to be practicing some sort of foreign script as he lay in bed.

I met with the doctor who had examined him, and he recommended a specialist in our hospital who might be able to treat Pan. Another student of mine arranged an introduction, and I was eventually able to set up an appointment. In the meantime, Pan confessed that he had had these pains for several years but had never found the time to do anything about it. He asked me to accompany him to the hospital to make the proper introductions, but once he met the doctor, he asked me to leave.

I didn't see him for several weeks after that. I happened to bump into the doctor on the street, though, and thanked him for seeing Pan so quickly. He smiled, and said that it was no trouble, but that he was afraid he wouldn't be of much help. Pan suffered from an ulcer, a gall bladder disorder, heart disease, and a fourth problem that I didn't understand, and he refused to stay in the hospital for rest and treatment. When I saw Pan next I asked why he would not stay in the hospital. He replied that the National Competition was only a few months away, and that if he left to sleep in the hospital for a few months, the athletes would lose heart. "I'm their trainer. I said I would take them to the Nationals, and I will." He did not mention his illness or the hospital again.

During winter break of my second year I did not travel, choosing to stay in Hunan to practice wushu. I thought Pan would be there the whole time, but the day before the break he was called away. I stayed anyway, and held to a ten-hour-a-day practice schedule, hoping that he might return before vacation ended. Four weeks passed, which I spent in front of our house drilling, or in back of the house hitting a sandbag propped against the wall. The morning of the last day of the break, I spun around with the staff, slipped on some ice and fell down. I twisted my knee somehow and lay biting my tongue for a few minutes. It had started snowing not long before, so at least the scene around me was pleasant. I turned around and noticed Pan standing at the gate of our little compound. He walked over, helped me up and looked at me for a long time.

"Don't you know it's snowing out?" he finally asked.

"Yes . . ."

"Then why are you practicing?" It seemed an odd question, coming from him, so I didn't bother to answer. We went inside and I boiled some water for tea. He answered my questions about his trip absent-mindedly, then left.

Winter turned to spring, and by May Changsha was sweltering again. Instead of slipping on patches of ice, I was splashing around in the puddles I made by dumping buckets of water over my head every few minutes to keep cool. Since that day in winter I hadn't seen Pan much, except when he came to adjust and correct the repertoire I was learning from my other teachers. One day he interrupted our session and asked me to sit down for a while. We went inside, sat down, and he became very serious.

"We don't have much time. Just a few months. I don't have time for English anymore—there's only wushu now. What is the one thing you want to learn before you leave? Choose it, and I'll give it to you."

I didn't have to think long. I had once seen him using, all by himself in the training hall with the lights turned off, a huge sword that he held with both hands. He only let me see it once, and laughed whenever I asked if I could learn it. "I want to learn the long sword." He frowned, then said very slowly, "Very few people use that sword. I've never taught it to anyone. And I only perform it for certain people." I didn't say anything, nor did I avoid his gaze. After an interminable silence, he pushed his finger hard against my chest and waited until he knew he had grasped my full attention. "If I teach it to you, and you wield it poorly, you will make me very, very sad."

Bill was a reader. Wherever he was he usually had some kind of relevant literature with him. On a trip to Southwest China he bought and read *Rare Fungi of the Yunnan Region;* when we rode a boat down the Yangtse River he skimmed through *Maritime Trade on the Yangtse During the Ming Dynasty;* next to his manual typewriter in Changsha sat a copy of *The History of Moveable Type*—all in Chinese, no less. When he and I traveled to Hangzhou, he brought along *Myths, Stories, Facts and Anecdotes About Hangzhou.* Whenever we came upon a historical site, Bill managed to find reference to it in that book. For example, we found a huge stone with a poetic couplet carved on it. The couplet went something like this:

Sky sky earth earth rock rock water water
Green green swift swift drop drop rainbow rainbow."

"And the truly spellbinding thing about this couplet," Bill read aloud from the book, "is that it can be read backwards." In a bamboo garden we stumbled on a sign that indicated that the bamboo in that particular grove was important. After only a few minutes of searching under "Facts," Bill found out why: "This variety of bamboo was long considered extinct. In the middle of this century, however, a team of Chinese scientists discovered specimens of it in a remote area of Zhejiang Province. This discovery shook the world."

Having enriched ourselves with this sort of information all day, we found that by evening we both felt terribly sleepy.

Back in our room in the Hangzhou Hotel, Bill stayed awake reading *Strange Rock Formations of the Lake Tai Region*. I didn't have a book with me, so I decided to wander around the hotel.

On the ground floor a string of flashing Christmas lights over a doorway caught my eye. I walked over and saw, under the lights, a sign saying "Coffee Shop." The thought of coffee excited me so much I jogged through the entrance, startling the young *fuwuyuan*—service person—sitting at a desk just inside the door, reading a comic book. I smiled at her. "You have coffee here?" She tossed her head back and replied, "It says Coffee Shop, doesn't it?" I wasn't going to let her spoil my mood, so I walked quietly past her into the cafe. "Stop!" she barked. I turned around; without looking up from her comic book she said, "Five dollars. Entrance fee." "Five dollars to get in?" She pointed to a paper sign on the desk that announced: DANCING PARTY AT 9:00. ENTRANCE FEE: FIVE YUAN FOREIGN CURRENCY.

"Oh, but I'm not here for the party—I just want a cup of coffee, then I'll leave right away." "Doesn't matter. Five dollars." "But it's only 7:15—the party hasn't started yet. . . ." She didn't answer this time, just stuck her palm out and tapped her foot impatiently. I felt my face getting hot but managed to keep my voice calm. "Well, if that's the rule, I won't break it. Can I buy a cup of coffee to go?" "Nope. The cups can't leave the restaurant." I didn't say anything, hoping that curiosity would get the better of her and force her to look at me, but the magazine held her attention. There was nothing to be done. I walked out of the shop burning with frustration. On the way back to my room, though, I suddenly had an idea—why not get my metal travel mug out of my duffel bag and ask her simply to fill it. That way I could have my coffee in bed and enjoy it all the more. When I got to the room, I saw that one of the other four men sharing the room with Bill and me had returned. From his accent I could tell he was African; he looked about twenty-eight or nine and was in the middle of telling a story to Bill. "I tell you," he said, his head leaning back for emphasis, palms raised toward us, "it is very, very difficult. You cannot imagine, I think." Bill interrupted him to introduce me and explain that the African was a medical student in Beijing. "I am from Sudan," the man said. "In my country, if you want to study medicine abroad, your name is put on a list, and when your name comes up, they assign you to a country. No one wants to go to China, but if you turn down the offer, you forfeit your turn, and may have to wait years for another chance. So I accepted. And I discover, oh, it is true what they say. To be African and live in China, oh, it is terrible." He was a master story-teller, flaring his nostrils, pausing, and sighing with controlled despair. "Why is that?" Bill asked. "The Chinese look down on black people! They think we are animals, not people! I have lived in China now six years, all of my classes in Chinese, with Chinese teachers and Chinese classmates. In six years, oh, have I ever been invited to a Chinese man's home? Have I ever been invited to have tea? To a movie? Have any of the Africans? I tell you, if an African must live in China, he has a clear choice: he keeps his mind, or he loses his mind. To keep his mind, he must not think. He thinks, and oh, my friend, he dies. His mind dies."

Determined now to fight for justice, I found my metal cup, excused myself from the room and strode firmly into the Coffee Shop. "I brought my own cup," I said smartly. "I'd like a cup of coffee now, please." To my surprise she snatched the cup and marched into the kitchen without a word. A full ten minutes passed, giving me more than enough time to realize that I was completely at her mercy. At last she stalked out of the kitchen, slammed the mug of coffee on the desk, opened her magazine and demanded five dollars.

"Five dollars? But the menu here says that a cup of coffee costs one dollar!"

"Your mug is oversized," she hissed.

"There are five cups of coffee in here?"

"Come on, hurry up! I'm busy!"

Just as I started to see double, a last strategem came to me. "I didn't ask for five cups of coffee, miss. I asked for one." I put a dollar on the desk. She picked up my mug, walked over to a window and poured nearly all the coffee out of it. She put the mug on the desk in front of me, opened her magazine and resumed reading.

As I walked back to my room, my anger subsided, and I actually smiled, thinking of the fun I would have telling the story to Bill and the African. When I got there, though, the African had already gone out for dinner. Bill was lying on the bed with a book closed on his chest and his glasses in one hand. "You know," he said, "talking to the man from Sudan made me remember something." I sat down on the floor against the wall, drank my coffee and asked him what he remembered.

"It was in Africa, when I was teaching with the Peace Corps. During a break I decided to travel. I had to ride on the back of a truck for ten hours to get to the border of some country—I don't even remember now which country it was —and the truck followed a dirt road through a desert. In my whole life I had never felt so close to going mad. I thought I would die from the heat, the dust, the noise and the thirst. At last we reached the border. I fell off the truck, then stood in line for two hours at the visa office, a little shack in the middle of nowhere. Just as it was my turn, the official said, 'Sorry, closed for the day.' I walked out of the shack on the verge of tears. The truck I had ridden was already gone. I saw another truck parked not far away, so I walked over and sat against it, just to get out of the sun. Something I have to tell you—in some parts of Africa, people who own trucks often write something on the hood. It's usually something religious, like 'Jesus Have Mercy,' because a breakdown in the desert could easily be fatal. Anyway, this truck looked as if it would fall apart at any moment. As I sat against it, I looked up to see a few vultures circling, like they were waiting to see what I was going to do. My eyes wandered from the vultures to the hood of the truck next to my head. There, in white lettering, it said, MY FRIEND, IT IS NOT BEAUTIFUL."

It was an important day for the 1983 English Medical Class —they were to perform their first co-ed skits. It had been distracting that these medical students had not yet gotten over their fear of speaking with members of the opposite sex. At last Jan and I had assigned groups composed of both girls and boys and told them they would present their skits on Monday morning. When that day arrived, of course no one volunteered to go first. I pointed to one of the students, Duncan, and told him to gather his partners for their skit. After making all sorts of protests he finally stood up and walked out of the classroom. Then Alison and Heidi got up and stood in front of the class.

ALISON: "We are playing ping-pong."

They pretended to play ping-pong. Suddenly Duncan walked into the classroom, approached them, hesitated, opened his mouth, and turned and faced the blackboard.

DUNCAN: "Excuse me, girls. May I enjoy you?"

ME: "Duncan, you mean 'join you.' "

Duncan, embarrassed that he had made a mistake, turned purple.

ME: "Keep going."

The two girls put their imaginary paddles down angrily.

HEIDI: "No! Go play with yourself!"

ME: "You should say 'play *by* yourself.' You play with others, and play by yourself."

HEIDI: "By yourself."

The skit completed, all three performers ran to their seats, where they were teased by their neighbors. Just as I was debating whether I had the courage to hear the next skit, the classroom door opened and an unfamiliar woman led by Teacher Wu walked in, handed me an envelope, then walked out without a word. I opened the envelope and pulled out what appeared to be an invitation, elegantly printed in Chinese and decorated with several red seals. It was written in classical Chinese, too difficult for me to sight-read, so I put it in my pocket, braced myself and called on the next group.

When I got back to my room I took out the card and looked at it again. I realized that it was not printed but meticulously written out with a miniature brush. Whoever wrote it, I thought, must have spent hours on it.

"To Mr. Sima Ming:" it opened.

"Greetings to you. I am a retired professor who loves and practices calligraphy. I am a poor calligrapher, but I am nevertheless concerned about the future of calligraphy. I heard recently that a young American at Hunan Medical College was interested in calligraphy, and had even gone to the trouble to learn it himself to understand it further. When I heard this I was deeply moved, and hoped I could meet you before you returned to your country."

It closed with an invitation to visit and was signed "Jin Wenzhi."

I wrote back that day, thanking Professor Jin for his letter and asking when I might visit him. Three days later I received his answer, inviting me to come for tea that Saturday afternoon after xiuxi.

I brought with me, as he requested, a few samples of my latest calligraphy exercises, along with the models I had used.

The woman who had delivered the first letter opened the door. "I am Luo Binfu, Professor Jin's wife," she said. "Please come in. He's just getting up from xiuxi, so he will be a few minutes. Why don't you have some tea?" I had a cup of tea by myself in their small living room, noticing that huge, unframed sheets of calligraphy hung loosely over the walls, some overlapping each other and all blowing slowly in the wind of an electric fan. A few minutes later his wife came back and asked me to come into the next room. There, propped up in a bed covered with calligraphy manuals, rice paper and brushes, sat Professor Jin. His face looked pale and swollen, with patches of red across his cheeks and throat. He extended a bloated, stiff hand for me to shake. "I'm sorry I couldn't come out to greet you," he said. His wife explained that he suffered from chronic bouts of fever, headache and swelling caused by heart and liver disease. "But you see," Jin interrupted, pointing to the fresh examples of calligraphy on the bed, "it doesn't stop me from writing." He shuffled through some books in front of him, choosing an old volume worn from use and spattered with ink. "If you copy out the models of a particular master," he said, "you will be influenced by his personality. This is the model I use—you see how strong, disciplined and clean his brushstrokes are? He was an austere figure in the Song dynasty. His writing method strengthens me."

When he picked up my calligraphy samples, he responded to them in an unusual way. Typically, when I showed my calligraphy or performed wushu, people in China complimented me on the novelty of my achievement—"Imagine! A foreigner who writes Chinese characters! That's really something!" Compliments like that wearied me after a while and often reminded me of a remark I once overheard after a recital by the cellist Yo-yo Ma: "Isn't it remarkable the way he plays Western music so naturally?" Professor Jin looked my work over, compared it with the models I was using, then took out a red pen and started making corrections. "Not bad at all," he said. "The only major problems are here, where you don't finish the brushstroke with a sense of authority. They start well—you see, right here—but then get sloppy at the end." He pulled his inkstone and tray of brushes near him and showed me how to improve the strokes. Though he could barely move his fingers, all of them rigid with arthritis, he managed to wield the brush with extraordinary fluidity. He took frequent pauses to rest, wiping the sweat from his fore-head and throat, and closing his eyes to recover from dizziness. After forty-five minutes his wife reminded him that he should take another short nap, so I collected my materials and thanked him. "It's my pleasure," he said, "and you are wel-come to come here as often as you like."

"I wouldn't want to trouble you like that."

"Please! Why don't you come every week like this, on Saturday afternoons?"

"Well—"

"It's settled! We'll see you next week. Here—let me get up, I really should at least see you to the door. I've been a terrible host."

His wife told him to stay put and relax, she would see me off. When she and I got outside, she thanked me for coming. "He's been excited about it all week—I think it has given him something to look forward to."

The next Saturday he not only gave me a lesson but also presented me with a gift of several calligraphy books and journals. He promised to introduce me to a scholar of oracle bone script, the earliest known form of Chinese writing; this scholar could acquaint me with the historical analysis of Chinese characters. On Thursday of the next week, though, I received a letter from his wife.

"Dear Mr. Sima Ming:

"I am sorry to say that Professor Jin has fallen ill and is no longer able to live at home. He is very sorry that he cannot teach you for the time being, and hopes that you will not be discouraged. He enjoyed your visits very much.

Wishing you health,
Luo Binfu"

One of my students, Dr. Xiao, managed to find out for me which hospital Jin had entered. "Can I visit him there?" I asked. Dr. Xiao looked at me strangely. "But Teacher Mark, he is in a coma—what good would it do to visit?"

A Rat

A Night Ride

The Long Swords

"Let's look it up and see," I said to the group of students who had visited me to ask about the meaning of an obscure word. No sooner had I picked up my copy of *The American College Dictionary* than I heard one of the girls scream. I looked up and saw them all staring wide-eyed at my desk. A rat had jumped on it and was running around looking, presumably, for a way to jump off. With a great yell I slammed the dictionary down on the table. I had intended only to be funny, but by unfortunate coincidence the rat darted into the path of the dictionary and was annihilated. The students laughed and applauded, saying it was a magnificent demonstration of "real gong fu." On the spot they gave me the nickname "da shu haohan," Rat-Killing Hero, a play on "da hu haohan," Tiger-Killing Hero, the epithet of a legendary warrior. They had a wonderful time reviewing aloud exactly how it had happened and what it had looked and sounded like, so that when they told all their friends the story would be consistent. Eventually, though, something had to be done with the little corpse. I opted for leaving it on my desk as a warning to other rodents, but the students had a better idea: "Teacher Mark, there is a reward for killing rats! Bring it to the Rat Collection Office and you will get a mao (about five cents) for it." So the whole pack of us walked across the campus, with me at the front holding the rat by the tail, and my students behind me holding sheets of paper with the rat's crimes written out on them.

By the time we reached the Rat Collection Office, we had attracted quite a crowd. I explained to the comrade-in-charge where and how I had killed the rat, put it on the table and asked for my reward. He and the other men in the office laughed heartily when they heard the circumstances of the rat's demise, but as the comrade-in-charge went to his desk to take out a mao, one of his colleagues pulled him aside for a brief conversation. Then the comrade-in-charge took a few of my students aside and talked to them for a few minutes. At last he picked up the rat, tied a string to its tail and walked over to me. "I'm sorry to say that we can't pay you. The regulation is that the reward be given to students who kill rats in the dormitories. But here," he said, handing me the string and smiling, "why don't you take it outside and play with it? When you're done, just throw it away."

I thanked him and left. Outside the building I asked if anyone had any ideas how to play with the rat, but no one did, so I threw it away. When we returned to the Foreign Languages Office, one of the students giggled and asked if I wanted to know why they didn't give me the reward. "Sure—why?" "Because the other comrade pointed out that the official statement concerning rats is that they have been stamped out. Only internal documents, which foreigners can't read, discuss the rat problem. Since you killed the rat, well, there's nothing to be done about that. But if they give you the reward, then an official disburser of State funds will have publicly confirmed to a foreign resident that rats do exist here. They might have been criticized."

I couldn't resist asking the student if he didn't think that was a bit silly. "Oh, of course it is very silly. But the comrades in the office, like anyone else, would rather do something silly than something stupid."

"Teacher Mark—can I trouble you?"

"What can I do for you?"

"I have a relative. She is my wife's cousin. She is a doctor visiting from Harbin, attending a conference in Changsha for a few days. She speaks very good English and is very interested in learning more. Could I take her here to practice with you? It would only be once or twice, that would be more than enough."

Because of the overwhelming number of relatives and friends of students, not to mention perfect strangers, who were very interested in learning English, I had to be protective of my time. I explained this to my student and apologized for not being able to help him.

"Oh dear, this is terrible," he said, hanging his head and smiling sheepishly. "Why?" I asked. "Because . . . I already told her you would." I tried to let my annoyance show, but the harder I frowned, the more broadly he smiled, so at last I agreed to meet with her once. The student, much relieved, said he wanted to tell me a bit about the woman before I met her.

"Her name is Little Mi. She is very smart and strong-willed. She was always the leader of her class and was even the head of the Communist Youth League in her school. During the Cultural Revolution she volunteered to go to the countryside. There she almost starved to death. At last she had a chance to go to medical school. She was the smartest in her class, and she excelled in English."

Little Mi sounded like a terrific bore; I cleared my throat, hoping that my student would simply arrange a time and let me be, but he continued: "Her specialty was pediatrics. She wanted to work with children. When the time came for job assignments after graduation, though, some people started a rumor that she and some of the other English-speaking students read Western literature in their spare time instead of studying medicine. They were accused of *fang yang pi!* [Imitating Westerners, literally 'releasing foreign farts.'] So instead of being sent to a good hospital, she was sent to a small family planning clinic outside of the city. There she mostly assists doctors with abortions. That is how she works with children. But saddest of all, she has leukemia. Truly, she has eaten bitter all her life. I know that talking with you will cheer her up; you are really doing a very kind thing. When can I bring her?"

I told him they could come to my office in the Foreign Languages Building that evening for an hour or so. He thanked me extravagantly and withdrew.

At the appointed time someone knocked. I braced myself for an hour of grammar questions and opened the door. There stood Little Mi, who could not have been much older than me, with a purple scarf wrapped around her head like a Russian peasant woman. She was petite, unsmiling and beautiful. She looked at me without blinking.

"Are you Teacher Mark?" she asked in an even, low voice.

"Yes—please come in." She walked in, sat down and said in fluent English, "My cousin's husband apologizes for not being able to come. His advisor called him in for a meeting. Do you mind that I came alone?"

"No—not at all. What can I do for you?"

"Well," she said, looking at the bookshelf next to her, "I love to read, but it is difficult to find good books in English. I wonder if you would be so kind as to lend me a book or two, which I can send back to you from Harbin as soon as I finish them." I told her to pick whatever she liked from my shelf. As she went through the books, she talked about the foreign novels she had enjoyed most; among them were *Of Mice and Men*, *From Here to Eternity* and *The Gulag Archipelago*. "How did you get *The Gulag Archipelago*?" I asked her. "It wasn't easy," she answered. "I hear that Americans are shocked by what they read in it. Is that true?"

"Yes, I guess so. Weren't you?"

"Not really," she answered quietly.

"You are a pretty tough girl, aren't you?"

She looked up from the magazine she had been leafing through with a surprised expression, then broke into a smile and blushed.

"Do you think I am?"

"You seem that way."

She covered her mouth with her hand and giggled nervously. "How terrible! I'm not like that at all!"

We talked for over an hour, and she picked about five books to take with her. When she got up to leave, I asked her when she would be returning to Harbin. "The day after tomorrow." Against all better judgment I asked her to come visit me again the next evening. She eyed me closely, said "Thank you—I will," then disappeared into the unlit hallway. I listened to her footsteps as she made her way down the stairs and out of the deserted building; then, from the window I watched her shadowy figure cross the athletic field in the moonlight.

She came the next night at exactly the same time. I had brought from the house a few handsome picture books of the United States and a few short story collections I thought she might enjoy. She marveled at the beautiful color photographs in the picture book, especially the ones taken in New England during the fall. "How beautiful," she said over and over. "Just like a dream." I could not openly stare at her, so I contented myself with gazing at her hand as she turned the pages of the book, listening to her voice as she talked, and occasionally glancing at her face when she asked me something.

We talked and talked, then she seemed to remember something and looked at her watch. "Oh my . . ." she gasped, looking suddenly worried. "What is it?" "Look what time it is!" It was after ten o'clock—nearly two hours had passed. "I've missed the last bus!" She was staying in a hospital on the other side of the river, a forty-five minute bus ride and at least a two-hour walk. It was a bitter cold night; even if she was strong enough to make it by foot, she would get back after midnight and arouse considerable suspicion. The only thing to do was to put her on the back of a bicycle and ride her. That in itself would not attract attention, since that is how most Chinese families travel around town. I had seen families of five on one bicycle many times, and young couples ride that way for want of anything else to do at night. The woman usually rides side-saddle on the rack over the rear wheel, with her arms around the man's waist, leaning her shoulder and face against his back. A Chinese woman riding that way on a bicycle powered by a Caucasian male would definitely attract attention, however. I put on my thick padded Red Army coat, tucked my hair under a Mao cap and put on a pair of Chinese sunglasses, the kind that liumang, the young punks, wear. To keep my nose out of sight I wore a surgical mask, the way many Chinese do to keep dust out of their lungs. She wrapped her scarf tightly around her head and left the building first. Five minutes later I went out, rode fast through the gate of our college, and saw her walking a few blocks down the street, shrouded in a haze of dust kicked up by a coal truck. I pulled alongside her and she jumped on before I stopped.

The street was crowded, so neither of us said a word. Trucks, buses and jeeps flung themselves madly through the streets, bicycles wove around us, and pedestrians darted in front of us, cursing the "liumang" if we brushed too close to them. Finally I turned onto the road that ran along the river, and the crowd thinned out. It was a horrible road, with potholes everywhere that I could not see in time to avoid. She, too shy to put her arms around my waist, had been balancing herself across the rack, but when we hit an especially deep rut, I heard her yelp and felt her grab on to me. Regaining her balance, she began to loosen her grip, but I quickly steered into another pothole and told her to hold on. Very slowly, I felt her leaning her shoulder against my back. When at last her face touched my coat, I could feel her cheek through it as if my back were naked.

We reached the bridge and I started the long climb. About halfway up she told me to stop riding, that we could walk up the bridge to give me a rest. When we got to the top of the bridge, we stopped to lean against the edge and look back at the dim lights of the city. Trucks and jeeps were our only company, so we talked quietly before going on.

"Does this remind you of America?" she asked, gesturing toward the city lights with her chin.

"Yes, a little."

"Do you miss home?"

"Very much. But I'll be home very soon. And when I get home, I will miss Changsha."

"Really? But China is so . . . no, you tell me: what is China like? I want to hear you tell me what China is like."

"The lights are dimmer here."

"Yes," she said quietly, "and we are boring people, aren't

we?" Only her eyes showed above the scarf wrapped around her face, and they stared evenly at me. I asked her if she thought she was boring. She continued to stare at me, then here eyes wrinkled with laughter.

"As a matter of fact, I am not boring. I believe I am a very interesting girl. Do you think so?"

"Yes, I think so." She had pale skin, and I could see her eyelids blush a faint pink.

"When you go back to America, will you live with your parents?"

"No."

"Why not?"

"I'm too old! They wouldn't want me to hang around the house. They would think it was strange if I didn't live on my own."

"How wonderful! I wish my parents felt that way. I will have to live with them forever."

"Forever?"

"Of course! Chinese parents love their children, but they also think that children are like furniture. They own you, and you must make them comfortable until they decide to let you go. I cannot marry, so I will have to take care of them forever. I am almost thirty years old, and I must do whatever they say. So I sit in my room and dream. In my imagination I am free, and I can do wonderful things!"

"Like what?"

She cocked her head to one side and raised one eyebrow. "Do you tell people your dreams?"

"Yes, sometimes."

She laughed and shook her head. "Well, I'm not going to tell you my dreams."

We were silent for a while, then she suddenly asked me if I was a sad man or a happy man.

"That's hard to say—sometimes I'm happy, sometimes I'm sad. Mostly, I just worry."

"Worry? What do you worry about?"

"I don't know—everything, I guess. Mostly I worry about wasting time."

"How strange! My cousin's husband says that you work very hard."

"I like to keep busy. That way I don't have time to worry."

"I can't understand that. You are such a free man—you can travel all over the world as you like, make friends everywhere, and see places that most of us can't even imagine. You are a fool not to be happy, especially when so many people depend on it."

"What do you mean?"

"My relative says that your nickname in the college is *Huoshenxian*—an immortal in human form—because you are so . . . different. Your lectures make everyone laugh, and you make people feel happy all the time. This is very unusual. You should always be that way; it makes sad people happy. Isn't that important?"

I agreed with her that making other people happy was important, then asked her if she was happy or sad. She raised one eyebrow again, looking not quite at me.

"I don't have as many reasons to be happy as you." She looked at her watch and shook her head. "I must get back— we have to hurry." As I turned toward the bicycle, she leaned very close to me, almost touching her face against mine, looking straight into my eyes, and said, "I have an idea."

I could feel her breath against my throat. I asked her what it was. "Let's coast down the bridge—fast! No brakes!"

I got on the bicycle. "Are you getting on?" I asked her.

"Just a minute. At the bottom I'll get off, so I'll say good-bye now."

"I should at least take you to the gate of the hospital."

"No, that wouldn't be a good idea. Someone might see me and ask who you were. At the bottom of the bridge I'll hop off, and you turn around. I won't see you again, so thank you. It was fun meeting you. You should stop worrying." She jumped on, pressed her face against my back, held me like a vice and said, "Now—go! As fast as you can!"

Learning the long sword proved more demanding than any of the other wushu Pan had taught me. The morning after he agreed to teach it to me, Pan arrived very early with two broom handles, led me up to the bathhouse and began the training without a word. In the past, he had always told stories and imitated me with great humor to illustrate his points and to make me relax. Now, he rarely spoke and made no effort to be humorous, insisting that I simply drill until he taught me the next move.

My last month in China was a busy one, as I had to complete my teaching duties, prepare my belongings for the move back to the States, attend farewell meetings and banquets and begin saying goodbye to my friends, students, colleagues and teachers. Still, I practiced as much as I could with my broomstick, never knowing when Pan would come next, and always wondering what would happen if I "made him sad." With two weeks to go, he stopped coming.

I tried frantically to get word to him, so that I could at least see him once more before I left, but no one could reach him. Rumor had it that he was in North China, but why, and for how long, no one knew.

The night before my departure, I was in my room packing the bag I had made for my swords and other weapons. I remember debating whether or not to pack my broomstick along with the swords when I suddenly jumped with fright. Pan stood not three feet behind me, with a rolled-up carpet under his arm. He smiled and told me to follow him. We would finish tonight, no matter how long it took. I reached for my broomstick, and he shook his head. "You won't need that anymore," he whispered, and we went outside. We made our way up to the bathhouse, and when we got there Pan put the carpet down and looked around at the night scene. "You leave tomorrow, don't you?" "Yes." "I will miss you." I stood dumb for a moment. "I will miss you, too." One of the coal trains blew its whistle, and Pan smiled. "I will leave tomorrow, too. By the time you reach America, I will be home as well. We are both going home." He told me that after years of waiting, his request for a transfer back to North China had been accepted. He paused for a few minutes, taking in the view, then said in English, "Let's begin."

He unrolled the carpet and took out two long swords. He handed me one, and we set to work. I felt light as a feather, and time had no meaning at all. We were both soaked with sweat, and he laughed and told stories the whole time. At last we did a routine together, then he told me to do it alone.

"This is the end of your training. The last move of this routine will be your own, and after that, as far as wushu is concerned, you will proceed alone." At that moment, everything was magnificent—the night, the heat, the sword, Pan and I—we were all magnificent. I flew through the routine, and when it was done, I thought I had never known such exhilaration before. Pan nodded, put the sword he was holding back on the carpet, rolled it up and faced me. He stood straight and looked right into my eyes, and suddenly I was back in the training hall, standing at attention during our first lesson. I waited for it, for the critical moment of our duel. Then, very slowly, he spoke: "I brought two swords tonight. I am taking only one back with me."

About the Author

MARK SALZMAN began studying Chinese martial arts, calligraphy and ink painting when he was thirteen. He graduated Phi Beta Kappa, Summa Cum Laude from Yale in 1982 with a degree in Chinese Language and Literature. His senior essay, "The Silent Mirror," translations of Parker Po-fei Huang's *baihuashi,* poems in vernacular Chinese, won the Williams Prize for the best paper on an East Asian subject in 1982. From 1982 to 1984 he lived in Chang-sha, Hunan, PRC, where he taught English at Hunan Medical College. There he was apprenticed to Pan Qingfu, one of China's greatest traditional boxers, and also to several other martial arts masters. In October 1985 he was invited back to China to participate in the National Martial Arts Competition and Conference in Tianjin, where he gave a public performance along with the first-place winners on the final night of the competition.